Coaching Women

Coaching Women

Changing the System not the Person

Geraldine Gallacher

Mc
Graw
Hill

Open University Press

Open University Press
McGraw Hill
Unit 4,
Foundation Park,
Roxborough Way,
Maidenhead
SL6 3UD

email: emea_uk_ireland@mheducation.com
world wide web: www.openup.co.uk

Executive Editor: Eleanor Christie
Editorial Assistant: Zoe Osman
Content Product Manager: Ali Davis

A catalogue record of this book is available from the British Library

ISBN-13: 9780335251209
ISBN-10: 033525120X
eISBN: 9780335251216

Library of Congress Cataloging-in-Publication Data
CIP data applied for

Typeset by Transforma Pvt. Ltd., Chennai, India

Praise page

"This book had me gripped from start to finish. It's all of the following: a stylishly written analysis of why women in the workplace get stuck and side-lined; a personal plea to fix the system not the women, a bonus-basket of idea for coaches about how to coach women, and men, through career transitions and glitches. It had me constantly jotting down references to books and to coaching tools – and I've been in the business for as long as Geraldine has. Some of it challenged my thinking, all of it entertained and interested me. A must read for any coach."

Jenny Rogers, Executive coach, Author of Are You Listening? and Coaching Skills: the definitive guide to being a coach

"Geraldine Gallacher's book makes a valuable contribution to the debate about the future of coaching in a challenged world. The author throws important light on what it means to coach individuals while taking account of the unequal system in which they operate. She highlights how a preoccupation with impartiality risks collusion with this system and proposes that we help clients to be agents of change through our coaching. This concise and honest book is relevant not only for coaches but for corporate leaders and professional coaching bodies - and for men as well as women!

Alison Maitland, Coach and Co-Author of INdivisible: Radically rethinking inclusion for sustainable business results

In memory of my mum Teresa Gallacher (1937–2020)
and to the next generation of women in the family
-Georgie, Julie and Rebecca.

Contents

Acknowledgements

It's taken 4 years to bring this book to fruition. I decided to write it in the course of holidays and weekends mostly and so it has taken over my life in ways that my family and friends are only too aware of. My thanks go out to them for their patience and support. A huge thank you to my husband Mike Sell who has cooked for me throughout, provided endless cups of tea and a listening ear when needed. His belief in my ability to write the book was unwavering and he provided sound advice at key points when I was stuck. Thank you to my son Cameron Sell who read the Engaging Men chapter and provided very perceptive feedback.

I'm indebted to my amazing team at ECC who kept the ship steering in the right direction during 2021, a tough year all round, allowing me the time and mental space to focus on the book. I am fortunate to be surrounded by colleagues who are not only themselves talented and experienced coaches but also share the same vision of a more inclusive world as I do. I'm very grateful to them for reading draft chapters and offering very constructive commentary.

A special thanks goes to my Insights team; to Michelle Weston for her clear thinking and to Kelly Hart for her patient assistance with referencing. Thanks are also due to my editors at Open University Press Zoe Osman and Laura Pacey whose feedback has improved the book and whose encouragement kept me going.

The book is based on the stories of the many amazing women I've coached since setting up ECC in 1994 and also from the interviews I conducted in 2020 and 2021. I've learned from all of them and I hope I've done justice to their experiences.

Part 1

1 The gender landscape

I would like to think that the dearth of women leaders still affecting society at large is so obvious that I no longer need to make the case for more women leaders. It would be good to feel the same about the need for a book on coaching women. However, a couple of recent conversations gave me pause for thought. When interviewing a male CEO for this book I enquired what he thought lay behind the shortage of women leaders and his reply surprised me. 'Do you think that's still the case? It's not my experience.' It's true his own board reflected a 50:50 male/female split, which perhaps explained his opinion. Another conversation with the son of a friend who works in media also revealed that he felt my information might be a tad '*out of touch*' because his own experience didn't bear out what I was saying, i.e. that there are still too few women at the top. Both his boss and her boss were women, which clearly influenced his perception.

A quick online search after these encounters showed that, in the case of the CEO, the US Senior Team who were in charge counted only eight women out of a team of 26. And in my friend's son's business, the main board is 100 per cent men, although a new woman CFO is promised in 2022. Both isolated incidents of casual oversights you might say, but I think they are indicative of a problem I have started to worry about.

Are people getting tired of the diversity debate?

When I compare the research and news coverage of the topic of say, women on boards, available now to when I became interested in this topic in 2005 there's a most welcome improvement in the quantity and quality of available data. It seems to me that there is also much less blatant discrimination and that we've entered an era of 'second-generation bias' – that more subtle bias that's harder to root out because it's often not intentional. More recently there's been increased media attention on the subject of 'women's empowerment', more broadly in the wake of the #MeToo movement. Finally, there's a lot of talk about the need for diversity in company annual reports since the tragedy of George Floyd's death caught the public's attention and resulted in companies being quick to express their intention to improve.

However, I'm concerned that there's a lot more talk than action. My two conversations could be signs that people think that the problem of too few women leaders is already solved. Perhaps the public airing of the topic is leading to a certain 'diversity fatigue'? Might there even be signs that a backlash is starting? There's a growing 'anti-woke' movement conflating diversity, equity and inclusion with 'identity politics' and invoking a return to 'traditional values'. Does the success of Jordan Peterson's book *12 Rules for Life* (2019) worry you? Its first rule is 'Stand up straight with your shoulders back'. It seems to hark back to Darwinism and survival of the fittest to justify social hierarchy rather than recognise the impact of the system on people's fortunes. It is hugely popular with male millennials possibly because it eulogises a bygone era where men were 'real men'. I hope I'm being pessimistic, but these signs convince me of the need to restate the facts even if you are already well aware of them.

My first port of call is to turn to the Alliance for Board Diversity and their Missing Pieces series of reports (Alliance for Board Diversity, 2021) to check progress for women and minorities. The Alliance includes Catalyst, which 'is a global non-profit supported by many of the world's most powerful CEOs and leading companies to help build workplaces that work for women' (Catalyst, 2021). Catalyst has been doing research and advocacy work on this topic since 1962 and so I feel it's a very reliable source of data, even if the data does look predominantly at the USA.

As you can see in Figure 1.1, the situation for women has improved. It has gone from 16.9 per cent of Fortune 100 board seats in 2004 being held by women to 28.2 per cent in 2020 (Alliance for Board Diversity, 2021). In the UK we've fared better with FTSE women now holding more than a third of roles in the boardrooms of Britain's top 350 companies, largely thanks to the sterling efforts of the pioneers of the 30% Club (Partridge, 2021). However, and I think it's a big 'however', as was highlighted in the Cranfield School of Management's Female FTSE Board Report 2021 (Vinnicombe et al., 2021), the impressive increase in women NED appointments was not matched by a similar increase in executive roles. Only 13.8 per cent of FTSE 100 executive director seats were occupied by women and 11 per cent in FTSE 350 companies in 2021. Let's not lose sight of the fact that real power in organisations lies in the hands of executive directors and not non-executive directors.

For me, the pace of change is not cause for comfort at all. And the numbers for minority women are frankly appalling. Looking back at the US data, you could say that women of colour have doubled their representation on Fortune 100 boards over the period 2004 to 2020, but at only 6.6 per cent it is shocking when you consider that Black and other racial and ethnic minorities make up

Figure 1.1 Fortune 100 percentage of board seats by gender and minority status

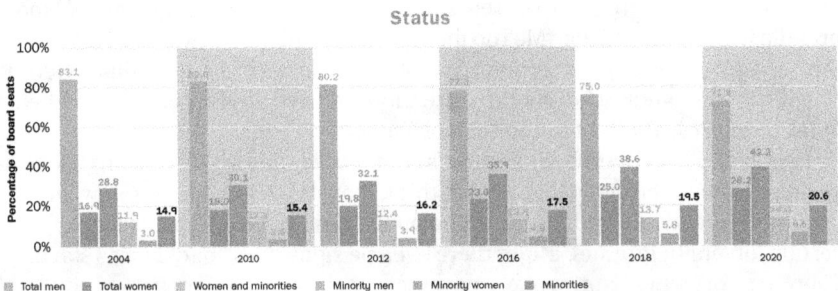

over 40 per cent of the US population (Alliance for Board Diversity, 2021). Here in the UK, the Parker Review in 2020 reported that 2.6 per cent of FTSE 350 company seats were held by people of colour and of those, 43 per cent are held by women of colour, i.e. that means about 1 per cent of FTSE 350 company board positions are held by women of colour (Anon., 2020). This compares to a 13 per cent UK BAME population according to the most recent ONS statistics (Anon., 2011), which unfortunately is the most recent census report for population by ethnic group in the UK.

This poor showing seems baffling when set against the data, which show the impact of diversity on business. To illustrate, McKinsey research in 2020, produced from a dataset of over 1,000 large companies in 15 countries, found that **"companies in the top quartile for gender diversity were 25 per cent more likely to have above-average profitability than companies in the fourth quartile" (Dixon-Fyle et al., 2021)** This was even more pronounced for companies who did well on ethnic and cultural diversity where they were 36% more likely to have above average profitability. Looking at the issue from the other end of the telescope the data suggested that those in the bottom quartile for both gender and ethnic diversity were **"27% more likely to underperform the industry average than all other firms"(ibid)**.

You would think those numbers would have companies salivating to hire more diverse leadership teams. But still you hear some cynics muttering that the correlation between good performance and more diversity cannot be proven as 'causal'. In other words, 'perhaps good companies can afford to promote more women and minorities?'

'Really?' I ask you.

Impact of the pandemic

My figures reflect 2020 numbers, but the indications from 2021 figures so far show that the diversity stats are not showing an adverse impact from the pandemic. They continue to move at the same pace as before but what has emerged are some signs of 'trouble ahead'. There is a significant increase in the number of women experiencing burnout, particularly mothers, as the stress of the domestic load (including the oft-dreaded 'home-schooling') and increased pressure at work collide to make a perfect storm. According to recent McKinsey research (Jablonska, 2021), three major groups of women have faced the most challenges during the pandemic. These are working mothers, women in senior management and Black women. Where women with very young children are concerned, the rate at which they were considering leaving their jobs was 10 percentage points higher than for men early in the pandemic. This was as many as one in four women considering leaving their job and now it's one in three. This does not augur well for the future.

I believe the pandemic has shone an even harsher light on the structural inequalities that have led us to the situation where we find ourselves. We are not making enough progress with respect to increasing the representation of women, and particularly women of colour, in business despite the very obvious lead that women have taken in education, with women having accounted for 56 per cent of the graduate population for the last few years (Marcus, 2017). The pandemic itself makes the case for a book like this one. However, to understand what led me to write this book I must tell you something of my own story.

A personal history

In 1992 when I was head of Group Management Development at the Burton Group (now Arcadia PLC), I watched a television programme featuring an American woman called Jinny Ditzler. Little did I know what an impact that television programme would have on the course of my life. The programme was entitled *The Executive Coach* (Ditzler, 1993) and it's hard to imagine now, but it was the first time I had come across an executive coach. The coaching industry was still relatively undeveloped, and it was pure happenstance that the first example of an executive coach that I came across was a woman. I watched her, fascinated, as she coached the CEO and board of a British insurance company over the course of a few programmes. I absolutely knew it was my destiny.

I was very fortunate that my job at the time entailed being responsible for the development of the top 300 senior executives in the company, and so I was able to practise 'coaching' this unsuspecting sample and learn my craft for a full two years after being inspired by Jenny. By the time I left to set up Executive Coaching Consultancy (ECC), I had already been coaching over 50 of the senior executives, chalking up an impressive 200 hours of coaching practice. I can't remember the exact gender split of my sample, but I do know that the vast majority were men. This was par for the course because, despite the Group owning most of the UK High Street womenswear fashion brands, women were only just making it into the top 300. The fact that my sample was made up of a majority of men completely escaped my notice at the time.

Fast forward 10 years and my business partner Kate Buller and I still had not clocked that we were mainly coaching men. It was only when Emma Spitz joined us after her second maternity leave, telling us that she may not have left the investment bank she had been working for had they treated her differently during her two maternity leaves, that we realised how pivotal this phase was in a woman's career. She was convinced that with coaching she may well have stayed on the leadership track, but instead she had felt side-lined or 'mummy-tracked' as it's become known. Her experience, and also her realisation that so many of the impressive women ahead of her in the bank had left when they became mothers too, formed the genesis of what we originally called 'Maternity Coaching' and later rebranded 'Parental Transition Coaching' back in 2005.

We were six years ahead of the Lord Davies report (Davies, 2011) that sought to investigate why there were so few women leaders. By 2011 we had already been working with companies to raise awareness of the problem and help them stem the outflow of women who were becoming mothers. I feel certain that Parental Transition Coaching made a huge impact on the number of women who, like Emma, left companies once they became mothers. We can point to substantial retention rate increases from those clients that measured the impact of our coaching – our clients saw their retention rates significantly improve post-parental leave, typically from 70 to 90 per cent, and for every 150 new mothers we work with per annum, we estimate savings of £1.2 million (ECC, n.d.).

However, as the figures above show, retaining women at this stage is not enough to guarantee more women leaders. More needs to be done. Attention has to happen at all stages of the woman's career and not just at the most obvious leak in the pipeline, when women have children, to ensure more women stay the course and make it into positions of power. I believe coaches are ideally situated to help these aspiring and existing women leaders as well as their male colleagues, to build a more inclusive environment for all. I'm proud to be CEO of a company that works with over 90 coaches internationally engaged in helping to make this happen.

Scope of the book

The scope of this book is based on the experience I bring, which is mainly working with large corporates and professional services firms. It's not purporting to embrace 'all women' but rather those women in these contexts. For example, there are a growing number of women becoming entrepreneurs and entering the gig economy. As this is increasingly a choice for women in corporate settings, I do touch on this as it's an important consideration for corporate firms wishing to retain and develop their women leaders, but the majority of the women I feature in this book are still in corporate structures. The experience of the vast majority of women in low-paid, part-time work is beyond the scope of the book but no less worthy of similar examination, as is a focus on women from culturally and ethnically diverse backgrounds, who are particularly under-represented in the cadre of women that we are invited to coach. This is an area calling out for more attention, as the issue of broadening the diversity of thinking in all walks of life is becoming increasingly important. This is particularly apparent in the McKinsey research quoted earlier, which shows that 'companies in the top quartile of ethnic and cultural diversity were 36 per cent more likely to outperform on profitability' (Dixon-Fyle et al., 2020).

Structure of the book

Part One

I have divided the book into two parts. The first part focuses on women's stories; coaching case studies and interviews with women at different stages of their careers. Through these stories I hope to show how coaching interventions

can be pivotal in influencing women at these different stages. The three stages
I focus on are:

- **Early career**: At this stage they are usually around 5–10 years post-gradua-
  tion and so in their late twenties and early thirties and hungry to find
  challenge in their roles, learning as they go. I had long thought the best
  teacher for graduates in their twenties was experience, preferring to coach
  people once they'd faced more adversity and change. But my opinion on this
  has changed since I've become involved in answering the question, 'Why am
  I coaching so few women leaders?' I'm now convinced of the need to
  intervene early when it comes to developing women leaders, because leader
  identity formulation starts as soon as people start their careers. I would
  even argue that it starts well before that, and my second chapter on the
  power of stereotypes will show that the absence of women role models
  makes it advisable for group coaching interventions early on so that suitable role models are introduced.
- **Mid-career:** This is where women, now in their mid thirties up to late forties,
  enter the busy phase, where the search for balance becomes more critical. It
  often coincides with becoming a parent. As I believe that this is a pivotal
  point for women's careers, many of the case studies involve women who
  describe the identity shift they experienced when they first became mothers.
  Parental Transition Coaching has become a 'go-to' resource for women at
  this stage to keep them on the leadership track and help them resist the
  'mummy-track'. It's also a time when women start to notice that the playing
  field is not as level as it first appeared when they entered their careers.

  It's at this point, at first appointment to manager level, that more men
  gravitate into leadership positions and women start to experience different
  treatment than their male counterparts. This is when 'second-generation
  gender bias' becomes more apparent. In Chapter 3 I focus on three women's
  experiences of becoming leaders and the strategies they developed to fit in
  while standing out. Providing a clearer insight into issues like the 'double-bind
  dilemma', where you're 'damned if you do and damned if you don't', when it
  comes to being more assertive, helps women to resist the need to change to
  fit in and instead encourages them to find their own leadership style.
- **Late career**: This is a phase in women's careers where they have come
  through the manic years, which often, but not always, involves choosing a
  life partner, looking after children or other family members, perhaps moving
  country and accelerating through the early rungs of management. They
  have now arrived at a place where their need for balance is still there but
  overtaken by a need to have their authentic voice heard and be recognised
  fully for their contributions. By now, their ranks of women colleagues have
  thinned out and they find themselves on occasion as the only woman in the
  room, or at least in the minority. It's a time when a re-evaluation can take
  place as they start to mind that there's an in-group and out-group when it
  comes to key decisions (Fine, 2010). They may also start to experience both
  the effects of ageing and unfortunately, some age discrimination. It can be a

tumultuous period of change and one where a search for meaning and the desire to do work that chimes with their values emerges and makes it a ripe time for developing another facet of their identity. Coaching encourages them to play to their strengths and listen to their inner voice and benefit from the significant opportunities that this new freedom phase can also bring.

I finish Part One of the book with a chapter on confidence. I feel it's deserving of its own chapter because it's an issue that comes up regularly when coaching women. It is volunteered by the women themselves, who describe feeling like imposters, and is frequently cited by their managers as a coaching need for women at all stages of their careers. As I believe there is as much myth as reality around the notion that women lack confidence, I interviewed women at different stages of their career, as well as some men, and draw on the significant research in the field to distinguish between fact and fiction when it comes to whether women lack confidence.

Part Two

In the second part of the book, I step back to consider coaches' influence on a system that results in too few women leaders.

- In **Chapter 6**, before addressing the question of how we influence the system, I start by stressing that when you start out in coaching you need to learn the importance of being laser-focused on your client's agenda. It really is fundamental to good coaching. However, I go on to posit that to engender the necessary psychological safety to draw out our coachees, perhaps we have to give more of ourselves. This can be in the form of divulging more of our own agenda. In other words, I'm questioning how realistic, perhaps even how valuable it is to always assume a 'no agenda stance' for the client. In my case, my agenda involves sharing my belief that women can successfully combine a successful career with a full home life.

- In **Chapter 7** I look at the systemic causes of too few women leaders and highlight that a lack of alignment about the problems may be hindering women from effectively changing the system. I then go on to indicate ways in which coaches can engage with the system when participating in women's leadership and coaching initiatives to ensure they are not simply 'pulling fish out of the toxic pond, hosing them down and then throwing them back in', to paraphrase systemic team coaching expert, Professor Peter Hawkins.

- In **Chapter 8** I make the case that to engage men in change it's better to enrol them in a shared vision of what the world could look like if we lost the 'women take care and men take charge' stereotype. Although apathy is at the root of some men's disengagement with the gender agenda, for many it's a lack of knowledge and the fear of getting it wrong. In the Daniel case study, I show how one leader conflated taking care with taking charge, assuming that the latter is how they achieved the former. By showing him empathy and respecting his truth, you can see how Daniel was able to consider a change to his style of leadership away from taking over towards taking part.

- In **Chapter 9** I introduce the counterpoint style to Daniel's 'hero-leadership', namely inclusive leadership. I describe the principles upon which it rests and the commercial and moral reasons for embracing it. Using a three-circle model of self, others and system, I emphasise how self-compassion is key to unlocking our capacity to be inclusive. I show how a tolerance of failure both in ourselves and others is a prerequisite for creating the psychologically safe environment conducive to engagement and innovation.

- In the concluding chapter I propose that to encourage more women leaders, we need to take a long hard look at the way we work today. I trace the history of the work ethic, which has resulted in 70-hour-plus working weeks that are not conducive to good mental wellbeing, and I look to the generation coming through to enforce the much-needed boundaries required for everyone to lead balanced lives rather than leave it to women to act as the 'canaries down the coal-mine'.

Who will benefit from this book?

This book is for coaches, HR professionals and leaders involved in the development of women in their organisations. It's not a 'how to coach' book but instead, using examples from my own life and coaching practice, it aims to furnish the reader with an understanding of what you need to know when coaching women. It focuses on the systemic barriers still facing women and brings these into the light to inform readers how they can influence one's coaching approach. I draw from my own experience of nearly 30 years of coaching both men and women as well as my company's experience of coaching circa 20,000 women in workshops and one-to-one sessions over the last 17 years, when we first focused on women's careers. I believe the case studies and coaching techniques I highlight are relevant whether you're a coach, HR professional or leader. Here is how I think the book can be helpful for each group:

- **Coaches**: If you are brand new to coaching, this book is a useful adjunct to a coaching skills guide such as Jenny Roger's excellent *Coaching Skills: A Handbook* (2012). I share the ECC coach model and many coaching techniques, but the book's principal objective is to make you wary of accidentally falling into the trap of 'fixing the women' rather than recognising the significant influence the system is having on women's careers and behaviours.

  If you're an experienced coach, you will likely already have coached women at different stages of their careers and will have, intuitively at least, encountered the differences you come across when coaching men and women and have learned to adjust your lens accordingly. This book will deepen your understanding of the systemic influences on women and offer further insights for helping women to not only navigate the system, but to also become part of the change that they wish to see.

- **HR professionals:** If you are in HR, the chances are that you are a woman (HR Dive, 2018) as is at least half of your client group. Even traditionally male-dominated industries are showing increased numbers of women at graduate level. However, when dealing with the highest echelons of your organisation, irrespective of industry, you will find your client group gender composition changes significantly to feature more men than women. This book will provide you with sharper insights to help you understand how that dominance of male representation impacts what's happening at the different stages of a woman's career as well as the challenge for you, if you are a woman HR leader, in effecting change when you are also in the minority. The book will give you pause for thought when it comes to considering policy decisions and some models and insights you can share with your client group to help you tackle the still prevalent issue of too few women in leadership and a persistent gender pay gap.

- **L&D and talent professionals:** For those of you involved in talent management and development, you will likely be responsible for leadership development initiatives designed to pull through more women and for hiring coaches for women at all stages of their career. The book will help you ascertain whether the coaches and trainers you are employing have enough of a nuanced grasp of the issues facing women to be able to coach them sufficiently sensitively, alive to a systemic approach to their development. I also bring to light how understanding difference is not only a 'must have' for coaches but also for future-proofing your leaders.

- **D&I professionals:** You will find the case studies and coaching insights helpful in determining your diversity strategies, ensuring they incorporate a fuller understanding of the psychological journey for women and recognise that one size doesn't fit all. The book also highlights that all diversity strategies succeed or fail by dint of the involvement of the leadership team and identifies ways in which you can engage more men in the drive for more diverse teams.

- **Leaders:** If you are a leader and you have picked up this book, I see that as evidence of an interest in developing more women leaders. As well as providing pointers to some of the barriers and second-generation bias that women experience, this book will describe a new framing of the role of the leader – one which puts inclusion at its heart and paves the way for ensuring more women stay on the leadership track.

2 The power of stereotypes

It's hard to write a book about gender without referring to stereotypes. Stereotypes are a cognitive shortcut. We use them to make sense of our world. It's helpful to be able to draw neat conclusions about groups of people to help us more quickly navigate the world around us. It's normal. But it's not inevitable. We need to be aware of them, of our unconscious bias, of the filter through which we all see the world. Generalisations, while helpful in summarising similarities, can be harmful because they obscure differences.

To understand how we make stereotypical associations, I found it helpful to delve into the research about gender differences. I started with Cordelia Fine's books *Delusions of Gender* (2010) and *Testosterone Rex* (2017). She takes an academic approach to the science of gender differences and looks in detail at the significant body of research that attempts to point out differences between genders. She highlights that although very little gender difference has been perceived in the structure of babies' brains when they are born, once those brains interact with their environment, they are exposed to the gender binary immediately. She draws attention to one study (Fine, 2010) that shows how mothers interact differently to baby girls and boys. I could relate to the experiment that showed that women talk and interact more with baby girls than to baby boys as young as six months. My own mother, whose own experience of parenting was conditioned by her having had three girls before my younger brother came along, once mentioned to me that I didn't talk enough to Cameron, my son, when I was changing his nappy! Perhaps she was subconsciously comparing me to her own experience? The research that Fine's book is referring to certainly observed that that was the case – women did interact more with baby girls than baby boys. So, I ask myself, are babies already picking up gender cues about talking even from mothers like me who are keen to raise children in a gender-neutral way? Another experiment shown in a BBC video (2017) involved changing babies' clothes and names to confuse the adults who were given the task of playing with the babies and given a 'random' assortment of baby toys. It elicited quite an astonishing difference in response. The 'boys' (who were actually girls) were offered toys like puzzles or ones that develop spatial awareness, whereas the babies that were dressed to look like girls were repeatedly offered dolls or cuddly toys and encouraged to play with them. By three years old, researchers have picked up gender differences in the way infant boys and girls play (Hanish and Fabes, 2014).

The debate about whether gender is a social construct or whether it's written in the genes – Simon Baron-Cohen and his essentialist argument – rumbles on

(Baron-Cohen, 2012). Full disclosure: I definitely gravitate to the nurture camp and believe that what constitutes gender differences in behaviour are often not biologically pre-determined but instead are largely decreed by the gendered world in which we are born. We know enough about neuroplasticity now to know that the minute our brains interact with the world they are involved in a dance between what they've been ascribed at birth, size, colour of hair, eyes and genitalia and what their context and experience brings to bear. Gender, to my mind, is not prescribed, but rather I subscribe to the school of thought that it's largely a social construct.

Irrespective of where you sit on the nature/nurture debate with respect to gender, I invite you to consider a particular stereotype that I believe has a significant impact on how women are seen in the work context. That of 'men take charge' and 'women take care'. the 'men take charge and women take care' stereotype (Prime et al., 2009) translates into people, men and women alike, tending to see women as the primary caregivers and men as the primary breadwinners. Young people reading this might scoff at the notion that this idea still prevails, they might even rail against using gender as a descriptor at all, preferring not to label gender, but my own experience of coaching women over the last 27 years has shown me how this stereotype still plays out in practice. It seeps into our subconscious from many directions and really comes to the fore when women have children.

Most of the women I've coached and those that I interviewed for this book feel that becoming a mother was a very significant milestone in their career. I think it's a critical juncture and one that is deserving of far more attention by organisations keen to retain women. Fortunately, many companies are cottoning onto this and that's why they hire us as coaches around the maternity transition. When I coach women who are about to become mothers for the first time, most have not thought deeply about the issue of how caregiving and breadwinning would be split when their first child came along. Many also think that sexism is a thing of the past and underestimate the impact having a child is going to have on their careers.

As Hettie Einzeg says in her book The Future of Coaching (2017), 'gender stereotypes may seem stilted and outdated but they continue to influence our thinking at an unconscious level with an obdurate persistence' (pp. 229–30). I should declare my hand here. I think stereotypes definitely hinder women's careers.

I would like to introduce two women that I have coached where stereotyping had an impact.

Box 2.1 ALICE'S STORY

First up is Alice, an investment banker, American, and someone that I coached through three maternity leaves. Alice and her partner haven't conformed to the stereotype of her being the primary caregiver and him the breadwinner. On the contrary, Alice is the primary breadwinner and her husband works from home to allow him to be the primary caregiver of their three children. I caught up with Alice recently to have her reflect on the impact that having children had had on her career. When describing the shape of her career trajectory she described how, at nine years, she had taken longer than others to make it from director to MD. Initially she had sought out something easier to allow her to be in a 'holding pattern'. She had, however, subsequently realised, partially through our coaching conversations and partially through her own experience, that that wasn't going to work as she needed something 'fruitful' if she was going to be away from her children. What we agreed was she needed more flexibility but not less challenge. She elected to go to a four-day week, and she believes that the one day working remotely actually made her far more effective because she was smarter about using her time. She was fortunate in that she had a highly supportive manager who believed in her and was responsive to the idea of her working flexibly. She found quite quickly that her career ambition reignited and rather than plump for something 'easier', which had been her initial thought, she decided to take a stretch role instead. This role involved a weekly commute to another European capital city. Three of her colleagues decided that they would also do the international commute. The other three were men. Alice felt she got a different reaction than her male colleagues, also parents, who had elected to do the same thing.

Unconscious bias

It's very rewarding to see how Alice has grown through this time and I sincerely believe that becoming a mother has significantly enhanced Alice's leadership abilities, which is something that I don't think is credited enough when it comes to considering leadership potential. Her story, however, wasn't all roses. She suffered from others' stereotyping at times on the journey. When she took the overseas assignment, she said,

> I definitely got a stronger reaction. People were just more surprised that I was doing it. So somehow for the men, it was no big deal to be away from home mid-week. But for me it was a big deal. Actually, I thought that was to their detriment because I thought they were making big sacrifices as well. But people thought it was more normal.

She didn't see this as a negative experience, but where Alice did feel victim to negative stereotyping, however, was at the school of her middle child, where her son was having a rough time. The teacher, herself a working mother, intimated that she thought that Alice's travel schedule was having an impact on her son.

> And so, I was a bit you know upset about this. I just wondered if she ever would have said that to a father if they were away a lot for work because I think that affects them too. I thought, she's a working mom. I couldn't believe she said it to me. I think that's why it took me back a little bit.

This is one of many examples of women being faced with discriminatory comments that can undermine their confidence that they are doing the right thing and have made the right choices. What's interesting in Alice's case is that the gender stereotyping came from a woman and her supportive manager was a man. So, it's simplistic to imagine negative gender stereotypes are only held by men. We all hold stereotypes in our heads and these colour our perspectives. In Alice's case she was able to brush off the teacher's comments, no doubt in part due to the support she was getting at work and also having a highly supportive partner at home who was the primary carer. If your support system isn't all hunky-dory, then a comment like that can be the last straw for some women.

Dual career couples

The way Alice and her husband split their responsibilities is still relatively unusual, despite the huge rise in dual career couples. In her excellent book *Couples that Work* (2019), INSEAD's Jennifer Petriglieri introduces three modi operandi when it comes to splitting the caregiving and breadwinning:

1   Traditional primary carer and secondary carer.
2   Turn taking where one steps back a bit as the other really focuses on their career.
3   Equal split of caregiving and earning.

Alice opted for the 'traditional' model of a clean split between primary and secondary carer but, less traditionally, she was the secondary carer and her husband was the primary carer. I would strongly recommend using Petriglieri's model with women about to have their first child as a way of having them clarify how they see this working out. In Petriglieri's Ted Talk (2020) she warns against women sleepwalking into being the primary caregiver and then looking back and feeling some resentment that their partner was able to continue their career undeterred by children, while they have experienced something of a maternity penalty. Much better to have a discussion about this up front. Indeed, we have created a Couples Quiz (ECC, 2021) to aid this conversation.

An interesting sidenote is that Petriglieri contends in a podcast in which I interviewed her that the most successful approach, with respect to couples staying together, is number three, i.e. the equal split of caregiving and earning (Gallacher and Petriglieri, 2021). I have also noticed, albeit I cannot talk to a significant sample size, that this is the route that many same-sex couples go down, possibly because they feel less fettered by gender stereotypes.

I want to now introduce another woman whom I coached who, at times in her career, was both the primary caregiver and the primary breadwinner. It's a pattern I see regularly among the professional women I coach.

Box 2.2 ANITA'S STORY

Anita is a banker and mother of two whom I coached through both of her pregnancies. When I met her, she had already got her MD title, which is unusual for someone so young (I seem to remember she was barely 30!) and so definitely a highflier. For her, there was no question that her career had flatlined after having her children. She recognised that for some women they could combine both, but for her it just wasn't possible. She and her partner, a dual career couple, had opted for the traditional roles with her as primary carer and him as secondary carer. She had taken 14 months off with each child and felt she'd benefitted hugely from this time with her children. However, she was for much of the time also the primary breadwinner and I believe this joint role was hugely stressful for her. At the time of catching up with her to interview her for this book, she had taken voluntary redundancy from the bank and was looking for new opportunities. She was considering stepping back a bit. It felt like an opportune time to reflect on how things had gone and what part becoming a mother had played in her decision to step back.

Role expectations and the cognitive load

In my conversation with Anita, when explaining the tug of the role of being the primary carer she said, '*It's how you and your husband and your family unit adjusts to a baby and what's* **expected** *to happen and who's* **supposed** *to do what*' (emphasis added). What she's alluding to is the dance of expectations that all new mothers suddenly find themselves in. Parents, friends, in-laws all seem to have a vested interest and a point of view. One woman I coached told me that the biggest benefit from being coached was that I was the only person around her that didn't have a vested interest. She saw me as objective. (Something I'll return to later, i.e. how objective can one truly be?)

Despite Anita saying that she was happy with the trade-off, there were times when coaching her that I could tell that she really struggled with the dual burden of being the primary breadwinner and the primary carer. Although her partner helped out, there was no question that she was bearing the cognitive load. As many women describe it, it's one thing to prepare the kids' tea but it's quite another thing to think about ensuring the right food is there for the kids' tea, seven days a week. Much of the coaching was around how she could balance her significant work responsibilities with managing a household. Prior to having children she'd flown around the world at a moment's notice and that was just not going to be practical now and so she had to really think about the roles she accepted because of the constraints she described around travelling. You can hear her own compliance with the inevitability of having to be the one that desists from a demanding travel schedule when she said,

I've never felt comfortable saying to my husband, 'I'm going to travel with my work'. Fine if it's one week out of the year but when it becomes part of your job on a weekly basis, I think that's really, really difficult and I also think it's hard for men even if they are like mine, who is really involved and very good with the children.

I agree with Anita that it is harder for men to request more flexible schedules than women because they too are subjected to the gender stereotype of having to be seen to be fully career committed and that is still conflated with being fully present. Requesting time off for childcare when you're a man can feel career threatening. It's notable how much paternity leave in the UK dipped during the pandemic (Webber, 2021) when job insecurity was heightened. Of course the opportunity to be at home more during lockdowns may have reduced their propensity to formally request time off.

I think Anita also makes a good point when she talks about how her long maternity leaves had meant that her husband had never had to get used to getting home on time or the kids getting their homework done because she was there to pick it all up. I do wonder if there is a relationship between the much longer maternity leaves in Europe compared to the rest of the world with respect to this soldering of gendered roles between parents. The longer the time, the more 'expert' the primary caregiver gets with the child, and the more the secondary caregiver recedes into a supporting role and not a co-carer. I picked up a certain amount of resignation in her voice when she said, 'People just get used to the status quo of things. And it's quite hard to then mix it up. And sometimes you feel that you're being unreasonable to say, "Well, I'm going to take this job but it means I'll have to travel three days a week".'

When it comes to how I incorporated into my coaching the role of stereotypes and how they affected both Alice and Anita's careers, I don't remember specifically asking how they intended to split childcare – something I would do automatically now. I would say, as a guess, most of the women, when asked how they intend to split childcare with their partner, say 50/50. However, it doesn't always turn out like that. The statistics don't bear this out. Our experience of coaching thousands of professional women through the maternity transition shows a different pattern. Alice is still something of an exception and Anita's story is more reflective of the norm, i.e. her career started to stall as she had children and, as she pointed out, her husband got used to her being the primary carer because she took long maternity leaves. Women often find themselves doing significantly more of the childcare and domestic load than they bargain for. Statistically, women are estimated to do two-thirds of the domestic chores and 75 per cent of the childcare (Samman et al., 2016). This is notable given how many assume that everything will be split 50/50. In research carried out in 2003, Bittman and colleagues noticed a phenomenon they called 'gender deviance neutralisation', where couples where the woman is earning more work together to counteract the discomfort caused by breaking the traditional marital contract (i.e. that he earns more and she cares more), by the woman assuming even **more** of the domestic load. It's as if she feels she has to compensate for emasculating her partner. (My words, not the researchers'.)

Stereotypes really do run deep and often I find women sleepwalk into being the primary carer despite their best intentions to share childcare evenly with their partner. I know that there are many women who willingly become the primary carer and defer the role of primary earner to their partner and there's absolutely nothing wrong in that, but I have coached many who look back and feel resentful that they have given up too much. And I'm sure there are men who, in retrospect, feel they didn't see enough of their children and gave too much to their careers. I believe this stems from the conventional shape of careers to date.

Kaleidoscope careers

Corporate career structures, to a large extent, still reflect a world in which a career is shaped in an arc where we start out in our twenties, start hitting pivotal career points in our thirties where we move into leadership roles or take on international assignments, which is a very turbo-charged phase, and then tail off towards retirement. This is no longer reflective of how we live our lives. A useful piece of research carried out (2006) by Mainiero and Sullivan highlighted just how reality was diverging from this arc-shaped career. We at ECC have visualised the thinking that underpins the Kaleidoscope research to make it easier to convey in a coaching session.

Figure 2.1 Career trajectory paths

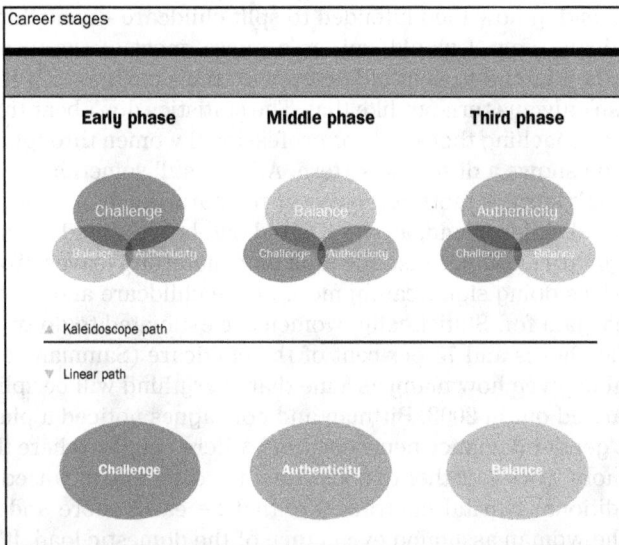

What Mainiero and Sullivan (2006) discovered, when interviewing leaders about the trajectory of their careers, was that a gender difference emerged that they hadn't anticipated when they embarked upon the research. To aid understanding, in Figure 2.1 we have separated their findings into two separate paths – Linear career path and Kaleidoscope career path. What they found was that men described the arc of their careers with respect to the linear path, but women described their careers as being more like a kaleidoscope.

In the Linear career path, men described their careers as having gone through three stages: the early phase was the search for 'challenge'; the middle phase the search for 'authenticity' (which was about making their mark and was the turbo-charged phase); and finally the third phase, which involved a search for 'balance'. As you can see, this does coincide with the conventional career arc which corporate careers have largely been modelled upon.

What was interesting, however, was that in their conversations with women in their study, they found that they described the same three stages but in a different order. Women, like their male colleagues, also set out on their careers with the search for challenge uppermost in their minds. However, in the middle phase the order changed and what followed, for the women consulted, was the search for balance. Notably, this was not just for those women who had children; all the women interviewed conformed to this earlier search for balance than the men interviewed. What came last in their career path was the search for authenticity.

When you consider the shape of traditional career structures, i.e. that you need to really go for it and give your all when you get into your thirties, you can begin to see the problem. Women were entering the phase where they wanted balance just when men went into their turbo-charged phase and, also, when organisations start choosing their future leaders! Very inconvenient timing. Just as most people are finding life partners, finding a home and thinking about having a family, i.e. a very busy phase in their lives, a huge step up in career commitment was expected. You can see how those in a partnership might be tempted to opt for one person concentrating on their career and the other stepping back and focusing on the home front. And given the stereotypical split of these down gender lines you can see how more men were coming through the system than women.

It was another important gender distinction, however, that emerged from the research which led to the expression 'Kaleidoscope Career'. They identified that women did not focus exclusively on challenge, balance and authenticity at one time. What became apparent was that women held all three in mind at all stages. This is where the name 'Kaleidoscope' comes from. It was as if at each stage one of the three features of a career would predominate but the other two, like a kaleidoscope, would not disappear but just appear tucked in behind, as you can see from Figure 2.1.

So, although women presented in the early stage as wanting the same search for challenge as men, they also, as sub-priorities, were looking for both balance and authenticity. For them, authenticity translated into work that chimed with their values, rather than making their mark. The next stage is particularly noteworthy. The search for balance may come to the fore, but it doesn't mean they don't still need challenge. As Alice said, '*When you're away from your child you do want a fruitful day*'.

In my experience, too many women are forced to trade challenging work for flexibility. I think this is very short-sighted on the part of organisations as it definitely has been responsible for the exodus of women from the leadership track. Hence the expression, 'the mummy-track'. They may not actually leave but their careers flatline, as Anita described her own career journey, for wont of better flexible working arrangements and greater predictability. Of course, the last few years where we've all been working from home may well change this dramatically. This can only be a good thing because it's such a waste of talent, as women in the third phase, when they search for authenticity, are brimming with leadership potential.

The research indicated that when their male counterparts started to look around for balance around their late forties and early fifties, women's kaleidoscopes shifted to bring the search for authenticity to the fore. As I mentioned earlier, authenticity for them meant seeking work that chimed with their values. It was about wanting to make their mark, to have their voices heard, do something meaningful, but on their own terms. For mothers, once the children had grown up, it was a time to concentrate on themselves. Neuroscience points to women having less oxytocin, the 'cuddle hormone', at this stage, which coincides with the menopause. Perhaps this results in them being able to push their own agendas more, unencumbered by the pressures of looking after others.

I should stress that the research showed that all women went through the phases in this order, not just mothers. The search for balance doesn't have to manifest as a result of children. Women sought more balance in their lives at an earlier stage than men irrespective of whether they became mothers. When women enter the phase where they seek authenticity, just think of the potential talent available for organisations.

Investors are beginning to see the opportunity of harnessing this potential and investment in products aimed at perimenopausal and menopausal women is growing (*Financial Times*, 2021). But sadly, I'm not convinced that organisations fully appreciate the power of older women and still too few stick around in conventional organisations. Instead, they join companies where work is something you do and not a place you go to. Where you are judged by your output and not your input – dare I say it, organisations a bit like my own. Organisations which harness this energy can expect to benefit from untold discretionary effort. I can attest to that.

Don't fix the women, fix the system

Prevailing career structures do not just fail to serve women well. They don't work for anyone who wants to incorporate balance in their lives. Organisations that continue to view a career as following the traditional pattern are going to lose more than their women. Mainiero and Gibson updated the research in 2017 and although for the most part it still held true, what they did notice was that young men and women alike were prioritising balance in the first phase of their career. Yes, the kaleidoscope now applies to all young people, regardless of gender. Balance is now primary with the need for challenging and meaningful work also becoming a requirement for young talent. Women have simply been the canaries in the coal mine.

Implications for coaching

I've touched on a lot of issues in this chapter that I will return to in more depth in later chapters. Here is a summary of the issues that are important for embarking on coaching women:

1   We are all subject to stereotypical thinking. It's a mental shortcut that helps us navigate the world. Having an understanding of your own views on whether gender is a given or a social construct is important when coaching women. I find more and more young women coming through are better educated about these theories. It is imperative that coaches really understand their own biases and preferences. A good place to start is the Harvard Implicit Assumption Test (Anon., 2011).

2   The choices we make when we become parents has a long-lasting impact on career trajectories and often women sleepwalk into the role of primary carer without thinking through the long-term implications of those decisions. Their heightened insight into gender constructs and expectations about being treated the same as men falter as they get to first rungs of management and especially when they become mothers. If you are a coach specialising in Parental Transition Coaching, it is worth acquainting yourself with latest thinking about dual career couples and, looping back to point one, it is also vital not to assume that everyone becoming a parent is in a heteronormative relationship and that they are even in a couple. Once again, always check your assumptions.

3   Acquainting yourself with the broader context of the changing shape of careers is helpful for placing your coachees' specific circumstances in a longer-term perspective. Mainiero and Sullivan's Kaleidoscope Careers is a good model for helping leaders embrace a more up-to-date understanding of how conventional career thinking might be hampering those who seek balance earlier in their careers. It's also very useful for helping women about to become mothers to look at their careers over the long term.

3 Leadership and the double-bind dilemma

In this chapter I'm focusing on leadership and the challenges and opportunities for women in today's business world. Having covered how our propensity to stereotype women as care givers affects women when they become mothers, I would like to now look at how this plays out in a leadership context. By using three case studies of women that I have coached, I seek to highlight the problem of thinking simplistically in terms of a feminine leadership style and a masculine leadership style. I hope to demonstrate that it's not helpful to solely associate women with a caring, nurturing style and men with a commanding, decisive style. I do, however, conclude that there might be some merit in considering the 'outsider mentality' that women experience and how this might be helpful in developing a more versatile, agile leadership style; one that's well suited to today's volatile, uncertain, complex and ambiguous times. To conclude, I outline the coaching model I use with all of my coaching clients and highlight the points where an appreciation of the context in which women operate is essential to orient the focus of the coaching.

Let me introduce you to Suzy.

Box 3.1 SUZY'S STORY

Suzy didn't come up through advertising the conventional way. In the UK 25 years ago, ad agencies were largely run by white men, with a preponderance of graduates from top universities, many from Oxford and Cambridge. Suzy's gender wasn't the only thing that marked her out – she had gone into advertising straight from school and so wasn't a graduate. Although this gave her many more years of commercial experience over her peers, it also helped to feed her 'imposter syndrome' – a feeling that she didn't quite measure up. She was also very aware that the prevailing leadership style in the agency where she progressed up to a fairly senior level was an 'alpha' style. Even those women who were her peers and bosses conformed to this style and Suzy, now a mum of two children, couldn't join in the evening drinks down the pub, even if she had wanted to. Suzy often marvelled at the arrant macho power-play games that her male bosses exhibited, and which seemed to work. The most powerful person, usually a man, would win the argument. But she knew these weren't games she was either equipped or interested in join-ing. Becoming a mother had many positive effects on her decision-making and focus, but these were outweighed by the negative perception of not being as 'always available' as her peers who had made the decision to prioritise career over home. Although Suzy got some recognition for her great people skills and her hard work, she was getting passed over for the big jobs and when a job she felt qualified for went to another woman who seemed to fit the macho culture better she decided to take a risk and join a smaller agency where she was the CEO and where she set the tone and culture. I stayed in touch with Suzy during this transition and although she continues to self-question and work extraordinarily hard to combat her inner critic, she has found her leadership voice and is blossoming in a role where she feels she can be herself.

Suzy's story goes to the very heart of the issue about women's legitimacy in the role of leader and the pressures to conform to a certain type of leadership. As far back as the 1970s, the tendency to 'think manager, think man' (Schein, 1973) was recognised as a problem, and yet today gender stereotypes still present barriers for women being seen as leaders. In a 2020 *Forbes* article at the start of the pandemic, Dr Abbie Griffith Oliver, then an assistant professor at Georgia State University, described how she replicated an experiment every year in her class where she asks her students to think of a leader and only 5 per cent of her students, regardless of gender, distinguish a woman and 'it's typically Mother Teresa' (Anderson, 2020).

Let me now attempt to summarise a huge body of research into gendered perceptions of leadership with the following, which I think gets to the heart of the issue. Leadership is associated with what are labelled in the research as **agentic** qualities such as dominance, having a strong opinion, being highly competitive with a real focus on winning and 'taking charge'. Qualities most often associated with men. Women are associated with more **communal**, affili-ative qualities and are seen as 'taking care'. This phenomenon, which you could call the 'Mother Teresa effect', has a significant impact on how women, and their suitability for leadership, are viewed.

Agentic vs communal styles

There's no doubt that Suzy's leadership style wasn't experienced as conforming to the agentic, socially dominant, hero model when she was in the original ad agency. Suzy demonstrates a much more collaborative, interpersonally sensi-tive orientation and often favours a more 'communal' style of leadership. She believed that the agency would actually benefit from a more collaborative, less competitive approach and possibly erred on this side partially to act as a coun-terpoint. Indeed, she received praise for 'being different' in this respect. And yet, when a more senior position came up for which Suzy was eminently qualified, another woman was hired from outside for the role. Suzy rated her very highly but the principal difference she noticed was that the new hire did fit into the macho culture. She didn't have children either and so was able to join the men down the pub after work. What was notable for me as Suzy's coach was the extent to which this not only dented Suzy's confidence, but it demoralised her. While working with Suzy to 'befriend her inner critic' as a way to quell the self-doubt that the promotion of this woman had on her and to have her believe that she wasn't at fault, what became increasingly apparent was that the wind had gone out of her sails.

Impact on confidence

I see this a lot with women I coach, particularly after coming back from maternity leave, who feel overlooked but start to blame themselves, usually for not being as 24/7 available as they had previously been prior to having family commitments. Suzy's morale got so low that she confided that she had started to look for pastures new. I find that when someone has lost their confidence it's a good idea to go for some interviews. Having the chance to talk through your successes is edifying and boosts confidence. Sure enough, Suzy's confidence did seem to grow after each interview as she could tell that her brand of leading seemed to be playing well to a different audience.

Danger in binary thinking

What was noticeable to me, when I caught up with her again a year after she had settled in her new role, was that with increasing confidence, Suzy was not only able to lean into her affiliative style, but she was also balancing this with a more challenging approach. Suzy's case shows the danger of pigeon-holing people in either a supportive box or a challenging box because with coaching we can adapt our style to suit the circumstances. Although research does show that most women display more communal qualities and men more agentic qualities, it's worth bearing in mind that it's not binary. And we are not restricted to one box. Indeed, later I'll get onto the topic of style versatility, but first I would like to introduce you to Milly.

Box 3.2 MILLY'S STORY

Milly is an Australian lawyer who has no trouble speaking her mind. I met her when she was a senior associate in a London law firm looking to make partner. Her business development skills were second to none. Being a rainmaker in a law firm is a fairly unusual quality. Lawyers are not trained to sell. Many want to be recognised for the quality of the work, not their ability to schmooze clients. Milly could do both. She was extremely client-focused and knew how to get things done at pace to deliver for the clients. She was a whirlwind of activity and having a baby hadn't affected this at all nor had it dimmed her ambition, although a few conversations with her mentor when she was off on maternity leave did worry her. It was no doubt well-meant advice, about making sure she didn't take too much time off on maternity leave and that when she came back to work to not make it obvious she had a child. Milly thought that having a child had hugely added to her life skills making her more empathic, and yet here she was being advised to play it down. What was ironic was that although her written appraisals were glowing about how 'she is simply brilliant at getting things done' and she 'has a rare talent for business development', she was also given advice about her management style and ambition. She was seen as too 'self-promoting'. Also, 'her competitive drive could turn people off, particularly when she challenged authority'. Helping Milly to reconcile these pieces of feedback was the coaching challenge.

Milly, unlike Suzy, did not conform to the communal, collaborative, team orientation profile often associated with women. On the contrary, by her own admission and in her own words she was 'decisive, assertive, self-confident, competitive and challenging'. Qualities she saw in abundance in the partners above her in the firm. The gender split of partners in city law firms tends to hover around the 20 per cent women/80 per cent men mark. So, in other words, city law firm partners are mainly men who, by and large, do get promoted on the basis of many of the qualities that Milly was being marked down for.

Double-bind dilemma

In the coaching sessions we focused on how she reconciled these contradictory pieces of advice: play down that she was a mother and therefore might be associated with nurturing qualities and play down that she was ambitious and might be associated with agentic qualities. I introduced her to the concept of the 'double-bind dilemma'. The double-bind dilemma is basically '*you're damned if you do and damned if you don't*' (Catalyst, 2007). Because the prevailing notion of women is that they are assumed to be kind, and '*motivated by stronger needs for nurturance, affiliation and succourance*' (Williams and Best, 1990), when a woman does not conform to this, she's looked at askance. As Sheryl Sandberg identified way back in her book *Lean In* (2014), a real problem for women who aspire to the top is that as they get more successful, they get less popular. This is particularly galling when their male counterparts have an entirely different experience. It works the other way. As they get more successful, they get more popular! The double bind is that if a woman shows strong agentic qualities usually associated with leadership, male leadership, she picks up negative comments about not being affiliative enough. However, if she doesn't show these agentic qualities she may be advised to 'toughen up' and may get overlooked as in Suzy's case.

Style of influencing – push and pull

I'm sure you can see the confusion for Milly. Was she really being too ambitious? Did she need to adjust her style of influence? I decided to use a very old model of influencing style conceived by Sheppard and Moscow (it has been updated and no doubt improved over time, but I still favour the original) (see Harney, 2021). It's essentially a wheel of influencing which divides behaviours into push and pull and makes the point that to be influential you need to mix your style between being able to assert crisply and be clear in your expectations (push) and being able to ask open-ended questions and good listening skills (pull). It's a model that works really well with all of my clients irrespective of gender. I have noticed that the majority of clients I coach are more on the push side. As executive coaching still remains the preserve of people further up an organisation, I believe that the prevailing leadership style in organisations does favour a push style. There was definitely merit in Milly developing more pull, i.e. slowing down a bit, canvassing more internal support, but only once she understood the gendered landscape that she was operating in and had a good feel for the double-bind dilemma. In other words, she needed to be reassured that the feeling of unfairness she was experiencing was completely valid before working on developing a more affiliative style of leadership.

Equally, Suzy needed to be reassured that her sense of failure at not conforming to the agentic style around her was also part and parcel of the same double-bind dilemma with which women have to contend. Confusing and sometimes contradictory feedback, such as Milly received, can be internalised by women and this can result in them not only leaving the company they are in but even the profession. Law firms are notorious for the exit rate of women. This is where coaches need to be fully au fait with the double-bind dilemma, lest they accidentally collude with the system and try to 'fix the women'. Highlighting for Milly the double standard unconsciously at work here was key to reducing the sense of shame I picked up she was feeling. She found it humiliating that she was viewed as 'self-promoting'. This struck me as ironic given how often when coaching women the very thing they are criticised for is not promoting themselves enough!

Code switching

A lot of the coaching assignments I take on revolve around leadership style. My work is imbued with a sense that the world would be a better place if we could recognise that although command and control has its place in a crisis, the complexity of the world we live in requires a different leadership style – one that engenders engagement and values difference rather than one that focuses on conformity. In Chapter 9 I will elaborate on this style of leadership, which is inclusive leadership. Here I would like to simply make the point that diversity is essential when it comes to corporate success. It is inextricably linked to innovation, which is the engine for growth.

Matthew Syed in his book *Rebel Ideas* (2021) shows the importance of using a pull style of influence to unlock innovative thinking. He highlights the benefit of having an 'outsider mentality'. As evidence, he points to the number of Fortune 500 companies that were founded or co-founded by immigrants. In December 2017, 43 per cent of companies rising to 57 per cent in the top 35 Fortune 500 companies were founded or co-founded by immigrants. Given that only 13 per cent of the US population are immigrants this is highly significant. Why might that be? Syed describes how 'deep familiarity with the status quo makes it psychologically difficult to deconstruct or disrupt it' (p. 141). It also makes immigrants more comfortable with risk-taking and they are likely to develop resilience and a way of looking around a problem rather than accepting it as an immutable truth.

Might we hypothesise from this that women at the top of organisations, still very much in the minority, might also have an outsider mentality? The outsider mentality Syed alludes to requires what I would describe as 'code switching' – being able to drop one set of assumptions and values and pick up on a different set. Might we also ascribe this versatility to tune into one culture and then another to women too?

Let me introduce you now to Athena.

Box 3.3 ATHENA'S STORY

Athena worked her way up the banking world from the age of 16 and, perhaps to her surprise, was now one of the top leaders in a large US financial services firm, where she worked in the risk department, when I met her as her coach. Athena seemed to cover all the bases. She pushed herself and her team really hard and was well known for her high standards and her followership. You couldn't help but be impressed by her ability to read what was coming down the line as well as her ability to be seen to tow the company line while still rowing her own boat. She was extremely data driven and examined issues from all angles. She had the knack of acquiescing to her bosses' demands while still making sure that risk was mitigated by ensuring her team engaged with multiple scenario planning. She noticed that her male colleagues rarely presented multiple options but tended more towards a system of advocacy where each jockeyed and pushed for their position so that what emerged was the strongest argument. Often the final decision was taken either by the most senior person in the room or the person with the loudest voice. This didn't sit comfortably with her as she wasn't at all convinced it resulted in the right decision, but early on she realised that this was the prevailing style and so she adapted to fit in. Her leaders wanted her to 'take a position' and despite it often having been the product of many hours of statistical analysis and the canvassing of many views she could see that presenting it crisply and owning it seemed to cut more water than using a more tentative, perhaps less dogmatic approach.

Athena didn't suffer from the double-bind dilemma. This was in part because she was canny in knowing where and when to use her more affiliative side and when to use her more socially dominant side. However, she also recognised that being an openly gay woman in a very male world was helpful. She had three children but her partner worked more flexibly and did the majority of the childcare, allowing her to match the anytime/anywhere demands of the job. She had moulded her life to fit into a system that was designed for men who had wives at home picking up the domestic load. Her male bosses didn't question her judgement any more than they did her male peers, which is a phenomenon that many women experience at a senior level – more critical scrutiny. She did fit in, but this came at some cost.

Sometime after I coached her, I learned that Athena had joined a non-profit and when I caught up with her to find out more, she surprised me by describing how much 'lighter' she felt in her new, all-women environment. Her friends frequently told her how much happier, more relaxed and fulfilled she seemed. She knew that the stresses of a regulation-heavy financial services world had been taking its toll and so leaving that behind was a big part of feeling 'lighter', but she also talked about the significant effort she had had to put in to 'covering' when she was operating at the most senior level. This had nothing to do with her sexuality, she had been out for a long time at work, but instead, she could feel she wasn't authentically part of this advocacy culture where the loudest voice, or the best argument won. In other words, she had to 'code switch' to fit in. But ultimately this wasn't fulfilling for her. She wanted to work in a more affiliative culture where ideas were worked on together more collaboratively; where it was ok to say that you don't know and where it was better understood that disagreement wasn't a threat to someone's ego; where tentative language was well received rather than assumed to be a reflection of insecurity. She moved to find a culture that fitted around her rather than stay in one that she had to fit into. It makes me wonder how many other late-stage career women might feel the same disillusionment with corporate cultures that remain entrenched in an outmoded way of leading?

So, are women better leaders?

There were a spate of articles in 2020 that pointed to how different political leaders handled Covid-19 and suggested that women seem to have handled it more successfully (see, for example, Zenger and Folkman, 2021). This line of argument might not be as helpful to women as you might think at first view.

I, for one, am delighted that some kind of analysis of the leadership styles of our political leaders is making headlines and I'm equally delighted that a case for more women leaders is being put forward. However, conflating the two might actually be harmful rather than helpful. By associating women with the stereotypical traits of nurturing and affiliation, we are reinforcing bias in the system not uprooting it. What women want is to be the leader they want to be. Men, sometimes less competent men, make it to the top because they can display either agentic or communal behaviours and are given the benefit of the doubt either way.

In drawing together the three case studies of Suzy, Milly and Athena, I hope to have illustrated the complexity of the barriers facing women in leadership positions. On the one hand you have Suzy and Milly, both of whom came up against the double-bind dilemma. And then you have Athena who, like successful immigrants, had learned the necessary agility to 'code switch' from one perspective to another allowing her to develop a versatile style which is well suited to our VUCA (volatile, uncertain, complex and ambiguous) times. Might women leaders, having developed this versatility of style, start to be recognised in order that they can become the role models for others coming through? Or might they give up on a system that seems to be changing too slowly and join other companies, like Suzy and Athena, where their style of leadership is valued and where they can flourish? Or will they start new companies where they can role model the change in culture they want to see?

What can coaches do?

The examples I've used in this chapter are women who were already in leadership positions and so much of the work I was doing with them as a coach was to walk alongside them as they navigated their path through different challenges. When I consider the methodology I used to help these women develop their leadership skills they do not differ from those that I deploy when coaching men. At ECC, we developed a model for coaching based on the GROW (goals, reality, objectives and way forward) model developed by Sir John Whitmore (1992), see Figure 3.1.

The GROW model seemed to us to introduce the goal setting too early. Our own model adds in context before we get down to the business of setting objectives. This allows us to help our coachee tell their story and consider multiple perspectives before zeroing in on their goals.

Figure 3.1 The COACH model

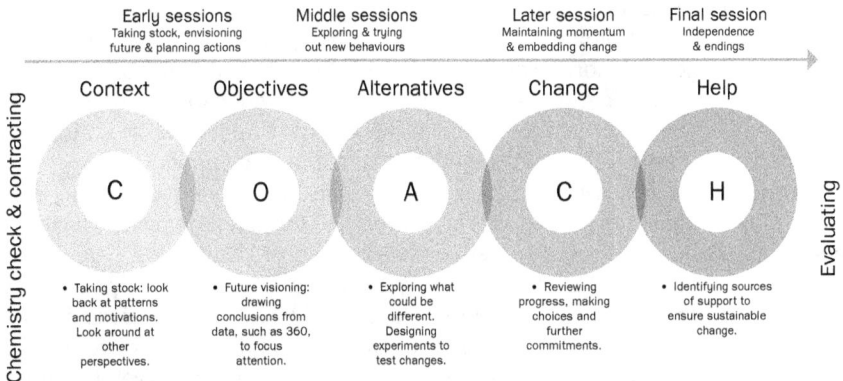

In coaching one must always be alive to the impact of the system in which the coachee is operating. However, I do feel that it's even more important when coaching women leaders, my reasoning being that too few women are leaders largely because the system needs fixing and so I'm alert for occasions where women are imbibing those faults and attributing them to their own shortfalls instead of recognising them for what they are.

When I think about how I coached Suzy, Milly and Athena I followed the ECC model of coaching which I use with all my coachees, irrespective of gender. However, particularly in the early stages of coaching, my questioning approach may reveal that I'm keeping a weather eye on the gender dynamic. Here I show how I might go about this.

Context

When it comes to the contracting session, I'm interested in how they lay out the challenges facing them. I like to ask, 'what brings me here to discuss coaching with you?' to elicit their objectives for the coaching and what they are looking to get out of it. I'm curious to get beneath the presenting issue for coaching and dig deeper to ascertain what's led them there. With women I'm interested in whether they draw attention to the gendered world in which they work. I think it's important to reinforce here that although the majority of my clients are in industries that are heavily male dominated, when I'm coaching at a senior level most of the women I coach are in the minority irrespective of the industry and so they are usually in the 'out-group'. But is that how they see it?

Are they describing their context in gendered terms? Are they referencing barriers to their progress that relate to the cultural context in which they are working? I look out for whether they are seeing their success and failures as entirely self-driven or whether they refer to extraneous factors impinging on their successes. Do they exemplify more agentic behaviours, or do they lean more to an affiliative style? When coaching leaders, I like to enquire what their vision of successful leadership looks like, who their role models are, and who inspires them.

I'm conscious of the stage of their career at which they have arrived. It's my experience that more junior women are less conscious of systemic bias and the older women get the more aware of it they become. But not all women. Those who have succeeded in the system often support it. I will elaborate on this later in the book when I discuss the concept of the 'broken bridge', i.e. the notion that women do not see the challenges facing them in the same light.

In my first session with coachees I focus on the 'lifeline exercise' where my client tells me their story. I feel this is an area ripe for picking up clues as to the coachee's frame of reference, their understanding of what's made them successful and their insight into the challenges they have met. The purpose of the lifeline exercise is to establish what characterises a high and a low as defined by them. I help them to see patterns that have led to highs and lows, and I help them to figure out what they've learned from the lows. Irrespective of whether my client is a man or a woman, I find the questions I ask tend to be the same. If I had to point to any gender differences in my experience of doing this, and I examined many of the completed lifelines from past coaching assignments to come to this conclusion, I found that more women name people in their lifelines than men do and more men don't include the personal line at all. But essentially my coaching technique does not differ depending on gender.

Objectives

At this stage in my executive coaching assignments, I involve the manager as well as other colleagues in a 360 review of how the person I'm coaching is doing. Often it involves an in-person three-way review with their manager. I'm super-vigilant in these three-ways for the dynamic between them. Does the manager favour an agentic style and my coachee an affiliative one? I'm fascinated by the interplay of gender between the parties involved in these meetings. I think it's crucial to be attuned to this dynamic and three-ways offer a great opportunity for seeing it play out. The 360 feedback is a potential minefield of systemic bias and also a golden opportunity for introducing the potential for double-bind dilemma that I referred to earlier. I find 360 feedback reviews have often resulted in the richest of conversations about prevailing cultures and their impact on the expected behaviour of the person I'm coaching.

Once we have completed the 360 review, we agree the objectives. Although these incorporate the manager's view because it's a critical part of the jigsaw, in that they are often representing the company view, it's vital that the individual's long-term goals and aspirations are explored first before we settle on their objectives. I find that women more often describe their goals in more relational terms than men do. Again, in my experience, I've noticed that their aspirations tend to be more holistic and their version of success tends to incorporate a wider context than men's do. Recent research (Sasson, 2021) supports this and makes the point that women in their study had more 'other-focused goals'. This may be changing, as I find myself coaching male leaders brought up in a different paradigm where there is more blurring between gender roles. The same study previously quoted also alludes to that shift and summarised it as: '[i]t seems that there could be some progressiveness over the years regarding gender roles in society. Women today set personal excellence goals like men; however, they do not give up the traditional roles and strive to excel in them as well.'

Only once we've looked further out and started to home in on what the person's purpose is do I then feel we can draw up some meaningful objectives for the coaching. I'll talk more about purpose in the next chapter.

In conclusion

I've known women leaders who have selected men as coaches to help them 'navigate the system' – the underlying logic being that if you need to be a man to succeed then you need a man to show you how to behave in a more 'mascu-line' way. In other words, if you can't beat them, join them. But that risks perpetuating the norm and doesn't encourage women leaders to tap into their own leadership signature and purpose, which I believe will ultimately serve them better.

I believe that a clearer insight into the gendered landscape facing them will equip them to better act as role models for those women beneath them provid-ing an inspiring picture of how women can lead authentically without covering, fitting in or, as it was described by one woman lawyer in our 'Women in the City' research (ECC, 2015), 'outmanning the men'. Intervening early to encour-age women to be the change they want to see is vital. If you don't start there you are likely to collude with the system and merely reinforce women's sense of not measuring up. For coaches, the mantra 'Don't fix the women' must be paramount whether the coach is a man or a woman.

I've focused on this chapter on three women that were already leaders when I met them. In all cases they had already charted their course to leadership and all three of them remain in leadership positions today, but they are still in the minority with respect to gender. What about women earlier in their career? How do you intervene earlier to ensure more women become leaders in the first place and how can coaching help? To discuss becoming a leader, one has to consider identity and so in the next chapter I'm looking at how you formulate a leadership identity and the importance of purpose when it comes to helping women step into their leadership.

4 Identity and the importance of purpose

I used to think that part of life's journey was the quest to find my one true self, my identity. But my experience has been quite different. I've realised that I have cultivated multiple identities over time – Scottish woman, daughter, sister, MBA , marketeer, consultant, trainer, manager, entrepreneur, coach, step-mother, NED, wife and mother all come to mind. Some of my multiple identities have even been in conflict with each other at times and there are still some that I've yet to explore – writer, grandmother, I could go on. However, I don't think I ever identified with becoming a leader. And yet I guess now, as the CEO of a sizeable coaching consultancy, I have become a leader.

This chapter is about how one forms a leadership identity, the impact of the lack of women role models, the challenge of competing identities and how coaches can help women develop their purpose to steer them into leadership.

So how does one form an identity?

Work identity is not a fixed concept, but instead it changes with role transitions. Every new role is the opportunity to try out a new version of yourself. When I switched early in my career from Marketing to Learning and Development, I was poached by a senior woman who invited me to join her in the consultancy in which she was a leader. I had been five years at the Ford Motor Company, and I had never had a woman as a manager, so when I was approached by her I think that a large part of the attraction was to work for a woman.

After a couple of years in consultancy I moved into fashion retail HR, where not only my manager was a woman but so were all my colleagues and team. Making the shift from marketing to L&D at 29 was a big pivot. I believe I was able to make this transition more easily because there were many more women from whom I could learn. I enjoyed having my first woman boss.

The process of experimenting and receiving feedback was crucial to that learning. The more I tried out running workshops and got validation for it, the more I realised this was much more 'me'. Those years in Learning and Development helped me to formulate an identity as a trainer, which in turn led me to focusing on becoming a coach. I didn't set out with a clear vision of becoming an executive coach. The coaching profession didn't really exist at the time I was making this transition. But as I carved out my career in Learning and Development, I began to notice how much more influence I could have on a one-to-one basis with leaders and then, when I watched the *The Executive Coach* featuring Jinny Ditzler (1993), I could actually visualise myself doing it. She became my virtual role model.

Identity formation isn't through reflection

My story is a good example of how identities are formed. We learn from others, we try new stuff, connect with new people, and each time we try something new and get feedback we adjust our identity and we reshape our story. Pascale et al. (2010) best say it as: 'It's easier to act your way into a new way of thinking, than think your way into a new way of acting'. The process of carving out one's identity is not as a result of reflection, it's much more about trying things out and seeing what fits.

As Herminia Ibarra puts it in her book *Working Identity* (2004), 'We learn who we are – in practice, not in theory, by testing reality, not by looking inside'. She breaks down successful role transitions into three basic tasks;

1 Observing role models to identify potential identities
2 Experimenting with provisional selves
3 Evaluating experiments against internal standards and external feedback (p. xii).

My story followed this to the letter. I saw the television programme where a woman who was an executive coach worked with a board of men; I met people in the nascent coaching industry; and I practised on many people and gathered feedback. In this way I could imagine myself being an executive coach. I practised my way into it. At this point, having moved up through the ranks in the same fashion retailing group over the course of five years, I once again found myself surrounded by men. My colleagues and my boss were men, as were all the boards of directors, and so I hung onto my virtual woman role model as a kind of guiding light.

It's only in retrospect that I can see how I gravitated towards women as role models. It was never a conscious choice. Indeed, I never questioned that my world was full of men, and I didn't appreciate how important it was to have people like me in leadership positions from whom I could learn. I also didn't appreciate how important role models are in leadership identity formation more generally. Skinner (2014), when considering previous research (Brewer and Gardner, 1996; Eagly, 2005; Sealy and Singh, 2010), noted that women place more importance on role models because 'according to the theory, relational identity is based on interpersonal relationships and interdependence with specific others, and women have been found to place greater importance on this aspect versus men'.

I was interested to talk to some younger people, both men and women, to hear about their take on role models and their interest in becoming leaders and to see if they were more intentional than I was at their age.

On the question of role models ...

John, at 20, doing work experience with ECC before going off into the world of film, was my youngest interviewee for this book and he described role models as:

> *mainly people that I look up to and I like their personality and that can range from people in my direct life or it could be, like, personalities from interests I have, like celebrities but they're known for behaviours I like or have a personality I associate with and are, like, a very good person. I like them. I want to be like them.*

John makes the point that when it comes to role models, we don't necessarily focus on one individual but instead pick up bits from a range of people, even those we don't admire.

When talking to Aiden, a 24-year-old in Fintech, and homing in more specifically on role models for leadership, Aiden jokingly said he looked out for people 'doing the opposite of my manager!'. Interestingly, noticing what you don't want to be is actually as valid and important a part of leadership identity formation as focusing on what you do admire. In Aiden's case, his company was predominantly run by men, given that it's at the intersection of financial services and tech and so he was able to survey a number of different leadership styles and choose from a number of role models to emulate, or not as the case may be.

It's a well-known aphorism that 'you cannot be what you cannot see' and it's thought to be one of the key reasons why it's harder for women to step into leadership. Women role models provide evidence that you can do it, whereas in male-dominated firms it's harder for women to picture themselves in leadership. When you are learning from others who are different from you, there is a mental chicane that your brain has to go through to translate those behaviours into ones that you can imagine yourself doing. This can really interfere with the leader identity formation for women.

When I left the car industry and then the fashion industry, I would never have conceived at the time that one of the factors that drove me to find new pastures was that there weren't any women in senior positions to mentor or sponsor me. Had there been more women in senior positions I think it would have improved my chances of stepping into leadership. I was so unlike the people above me in the organisation that I think the 'you cannot be what you cannot see' very much applied to me. Seeing Jinny Ditzler on TV doing the job of an executive coach made a huge impression on me. It gave me the courage and motivation to jump ship and start my own company and I hadn't ever even spoken with the woman! Had she been male I doubt it would have had the same impact.

Of course, just because you're a woman and in a leadership position does not mean you are necessarily going to be a role model for young women coming through.

Anti-role models

I once attended a panel event where one of the panellists was a high-flying woman head-hunter. The event was to talk about women's progress in business to an audience of young women lawyers. The head-hunter gave a rousing speech about what women had to do to get to the top. I was able to look around me and watch the faces of these young women and I could see the speech wasn't landing as it was intended. The bit that I remember is her saying that if you wanted to have a career you had to delegate all aspects of the domestic load. She talked about nannies and cleaners. I could see that these Gen Xers weren't identifying with this version of a life. I think that was the first time that I formulated the notion of an anti-role model. The speaker was unwittingly putting off these women from aspiring to leadership. She was painting it in unappealing and perhaps unachievable terms – after all, the cost of childcare has been going up steadily over the last decade and has soared in the last two years (Byers, 2021).

My coaching of women going through the maternity transition often surfaces the notion that many of the women at the top of their organisations are perceived as having 'outmanned the men' – a short-hand for meaning they are dominant and agentic. Some of these women, of course, do naturally conform to this typically 'masculine' stereotype (like Milly) or some have had to emulate the behaviours to fit in (like Athena).

Whichever it is, it does mean that many of the exceptional women leaders who have made it to the top are not seen as role models. It's an irony that you need to be exceptional to get there, but when you get there you may not be seen as a role model.

Do young women aspire to leadership?

Not long after I attended this event, we at ECC decided to carry out some research into young women's career aspirations (ECC, 2015), which I alluded to at the end of the last chapter. We invited our clients from the banking world and legal professions to distribute a questionnaire to a selection of their young women talent. We got 600 replies and the response was 50/50 banking and law, allowing us to make some comparisons. I think the most striking finding was that only between 30 and 40 per cent aspired to reach MD or partner level. We targeted women that had not yet become mothers so that they hadn't been affected by the motherhood juggle. But instead, we found they **were** affected by it because so many of them felt that the sacrifice was too great in terms of their personal lives to consider continuing in their chosen profession. As we saw in the Mainiero and Sullivan model described in Chapter 2, these young women very definitely were embracing the need for challenge **and** balance early in their career.

For this book, I interviewed a number of young people in their twenties about aspirations and leadership. I highlight below a few of their comments in the same vein.

Ellie, who works for one of the Big 4 accountancy firms said, 'I don't think I've ever thought that far ahead, (but) it would be quite nice to end up in a position of leadership, but it's not something I have expressly set my mind to achieving', and further in our conversation when referring to what might put her off being a leader, 'You lose your home life. And home life doesn't necessarily mean family, it just means you have to give yourself up to work.'

Caroline, a recruitment consultant, when musing on why there were so few women leaders felt that:

> *It's a lot down to children, women still being the primary caregiver. And then it's down to organisations essentially not offering the flexibility to do jobs in the way that, you know, if you can count on the fact that women, and I'm making a massive generalisation here, are going to be conscientious and do their best to get something done on time and to a good standard, then how they do it and where they do it doesn't really matter. I think a lot of companies are wising up to the benefits of remote working, but I do think there's still a long way to go there.*

Another finding from our Women and the City research (ECC, 2015) was that, rather than looking up to women at the top of organisations as their role models, they tracked the progress of women just ahead of them in their careers. They scrutinised those that they rated and were particularly curious to see what happened to them when they went off on maternity leave. They watched as many of them returned, often went part-time and, bit by bit, lost their footing on the career ladder. The ones that did manage to continue progressing seemed to them to have outsourced the domestic load but often appeared to have outsourced childcare too. In the focus groups we held, someone cited a story of a woman lawyer reading bedtime stories over the phone to her children from the office. This attracted a collective shaking of heads. They didn't look up to women like this as role models. They felt sorry for them. They saw them as anti-role models. The majority of the young women were not mothers, which I think is significant, and I will return to this later when I introduce the concept of the 'broken bridge'.

The pandemic has effectively been a global study of the effectiveness of remote working and many organisations have realised that they have been just as productive working from home as in the office. I'm hopeful that this will significantly improve the chances of women being able to imagine themselves as leaders, since so many I have talked to cite lack of flexibility as one of the biggest barriers to their interest in becoming leaders. There are, however, other unseen barriers that persist.

Defining leadership

As I highlighted in the cases of Milly and Athena, the prevailing model of leadership in the organisation also has an impact on women's aspirations to be leaders.

Since forming a leadership identity means experimenting with leadership behaviours, when women start to come up against the double-bind dilemma as described in the previous chapter, it can derail their first forays into leadership. If they attempt to emulate the agentic behaviours predominantly displayed in male-centric environments, their perceived lack of so-called feminine attributes are seen to violate gender norms and attract negative feedback, such as being described as 'outmanning the men', and yet if they adopt more communal behaviours they receive feedback that they need to toughen up. This is confusing and gets in the way of their leadership identity formulation. All too often women internalise this feedback and see it as failure to make the grade rather than recognise it for what it is – gender bias.

It's at this stage that a coaching intervention is essential to help them interpret sometimes contradictory feedback and challenge received notions of leadership. It's important to help them make sense of their experience to date, reframing and re-interpreting past events to demonstrate when they have already been acting as leaders. An interesting study carried out by Dr Suzi Skinner (2014) looked at the importance of gender and leader identity formation in executive coaching and concluded that coaches needed to have an insight of how leadership identity formulation differs between genders to effectively coach women.

Introducing a new definition of leadership to circuit-break women's received perception of leadership is an important part of women's coaching programmes. This serves to redefine leadership, highlighting the movement to more distributed and inclusive practices, which are predicted to be the leadership behaviours of the future. Behaviours that are more conducive to employee engagement. I was interested to listen to my group of 20-somethings describing how they saw leadership. Here are a few of the definitions preferred:

John:

A collaborative style – getting the best out of people because you're really listening to their ideas and to what they think. And almost, your role as leader is about knowing where you want to go, but you're using everyone's brainpower together. Not a command or control style.

Aiden:

Making sure everyone is happy and efficient. Providing them with an environment to flourish. Enabling others.

Caroline:

Working out the differences of those personalities that you manage and catering to them and kind of bringing their confidence levels up, drawing upon their strengths and making them the best version of themselves. That to me is a true leader rather than someone that kind of has a 'my way or the highway' attitude.

Ella:

Someone who has continued to learn and puts that learning into practice. I think leading is not necessarily telling people what to do. It's understanding people around you and pulling people up with you. And being willing to try a new idea or be persuaded to try something. It's about malleability.

It's interesting to note how consistent they were in seeing leadership in terms of a pull style of influence more than a push style. This more readily conforms to those communal traits previously described as more commonly associated with women. Some of them went as far as to flat out reject those agentic, take charge behaviours more commonly associated with men, actually naming them as 'command and control' or 'my way or the highway'. Highlighting this for women who are considering stepping into leadership is important to encourage them that change is afoot and the old adage 'think manager, think man' does appear to be on the way out, and with it hopefully the notion of 'outmanning the men' and the tendency to stereotype leadership behaviours as either communal or agentic. I look forward to a time when leaders of any gender can display either communal or agentic behaviours as warranted by the situation. I think Michael Kimmel puts it well when he says, 'Love, tenderness, nurturance; competence, ambition, assertion – these are "human qualities" and all human beings – both men and women – should have equal access to them' (Kimmel and Aronson, 2008).

Identity clash

When you examine women's careers there is evidence that they flatline at the time when they become mothers. They may not be leaving in the same numbers, but they are getting stuck. This is a key time for identity transition and it's crucial that women are encouraged to not think in terms of either/or when it comes to their identity as a leader and as a mother. Parental transition coaching is the ideal time to help women view their experience of becoming a mother as additive to their leadership identity and not an impediment.

At ECC we developed a model to track the psychological journey that career women follow when they first learn that they are pregnant through to their re-integration into work. We call it the VAST model, which stands for vigilance, appreciation, separation and trial. Coaching women through these stages is primarily focused on helping them knit together their newfound identity as a mother with their existing work identity and burgeoning leadership identity.

Vigilance

Nine months of pregnancy is good preparation for mothers who start to envisage their future selves at work and with a baby. They become vigilant about others that have made the journey before and seek out stories from others just ahead of them in the pipeline. Workshops that feature other mothers going through the process, facilitated by a coach who can provide data and advice as well as hold a space for shared experience among participants, are becoming the norm for organisations for women at all levels. Women further on in their careers opt for one-to-one coaching as they feel the need to examine and make sense of their own specific context. Going back to the Ibarra model (2004), they are seeking out role models and experimenting with provisional selves.

Appreciation

This phase is following the birth of their child and the practical reality of their new identity takes form. In addition to appreciating the new addition to their lives, they start to appreciate just how different their world has become. With respect to identity formation, they discover a new network, new connections and they appreciate another world outside of their work identity. In this local world of family and friends they find a new tribe – others with whom they can find psychological convergence. In European countries where maternity leave is typically longer, this phase can be as long as the Vigilance phase, i.e. nine months and increasingly 12 months, giving time for their mother identity to take root.

In the USA where 25 per cent of mothers go back to work after having their baby within two weeks (Kliff, 2015), the process of forging their motherhood identity has to happen more quickly. Statistically, the USA doesn't produce any more leaders than most European countries and so short maternity leaves are not the answer, but it is interesting to note that in Germany, where women are encouraged to take up to three years of leave, the number of women leaders is notably lower. It would be interesting to research what difference length of maternity leave has on leadership identity for women.

For the majority of the women we coach, the decision to go back to work is a foregone conclusion as many are in dual career couples and may be the primary breadwinner. These new mothers really appreciate the objective sounding board of a coach with no vested interest. We are a career handrail in shifting territory. At this point women are often besieged by well-meaning advice coming from multiple quarters and they use the coaching space to forge their own path, uncluttered by vested interest.

Separation

While this obviously references the separation from their baby, which is often, but not always, a huge psychological wrench for women when they go back to work, it also shines a light on the tendency to think of their two identities as mother and careerist as separate until now. Going back to work is part of the process of integrating and reconciling these identities. The coach's role is to help them re-validate their career credentials. Coaching the manager too is vital because it's through contact with them that the real re-validation comes. I find that part of that career re-validation is to reinforce that the skills they have learned have actually been a crash course in leadership. Their new inelastic days force them to delegate and prioritise more ruthlessly. I believe it also forces them to move towards the 80:20 rule, recognising that 20 per cent of what you do has 80 per cent impact. Without coaching, some women can attempt to go back to work operating under the same conscientious, often perfectionistic standards that they previously set themselves and can find themselves coming up short. Helping them to see that they have actually gained a leadership skillset while not at work is vital to re-igniting their leadership hopes. Women, especially those with perfectionistic tendencies, can find themselves inhibited at this stage from taking career risks and applying for promotions. I applaud those managers who are not put off by what can be a dip in confidence and put them forward for promotion, not succumbing to benevolence bias where they unintentionally slow things down due to feeling sorry for women returners. Coaching the manager is an ideal place in which to warn against benevolence bias. I expand on this in Chapter 8, 'Engaging men'.

Trial

As with any new facet of identity, what follows is a period of trial. In some ways after becoming mothers, you might perceive their future relationship with work as an ongoing trial forever weighing up the demands of their dual identities of mother and worker. This is a significant psychological challenge as women experience cognitive dissonance as their sense of self re-orders and they accept the multiplicity of their identities.

On a practical level, an important topic for coaching is addressing how the domestic load is shared at home. As I outlined in Chapter 2, all too often women sleepwalk into being the primary caregiver despite being equal earners. For many, gender inequity still prevails at home. I do see part of the role of the coach is to challenge that received wisdom, for example asking why they assume they have to do all the pick-ups and drop-offs, or the tendency to deduct all the childcare costs from their income rather than considering that childcare should be deducted from the family income. This at least encourages conversations at home about conscious co-parenting. I'm surprised through the parental transition coaching I do how often couples don't talk about this stuff. I notice how their decisions are being influenced by deeper psychological and social forces as I outlined in Chapter 2 when I covered the power of stereotypes. As Jennifer Petriglieri mentions in her 2020 Ted Talk, it doesn't matter how you choose to share childcare and the domestic load, as long as you talk about it.

Of course, it's also worth bearing in mind that women are lone parents in 22 per cent of UK working families with dependents (Oppenheim, 2019) and so the coaching conversation needs to focus on support more broadly.

Research by Noon and Nieuwerburgh (2020) describes how coaching at this stage provides neutral support and a conducive thinking environment to ensure the returning mother, in the possible absence of relatable role models, does not automatically revert to a gendered script. Also that coaching helps women navigate a complex period of decision-making which could otherwise be done in isolation, despite often being in a partnership. The coaching space enables individuals to find coherence and develop confidence in their decision-making. Moreover, coaching helps to remind them that they matter as individuals and the opportunity to vocalise concerns and intentions helps to crystallise action.

The importance of purpose

When women are navigating this tricky period, I have found that focusing on purpose is helpful to provide a North Star for returning mothers. Indeed, it's an important dimension in all coaching. When it comes to returning mothers, having them think about their reasons for working often results in them describing how they want to be a role model for their children, most particularly for their daughters (Carey, 2021).

Broadening out, developing a meaningful purpose is critical for all women to provide momentum to power them through often uncharted territory. I caught up with a woman banker that I'd coached over 10 years ago, and we discussed the importance of having a guiding purpose when your sense of self is all at sea.

Box 4.1 ELLIE'S STORY

Ellie was working in Switzerland when I caught up with her. Ellie is American and the father of her children is English, and when we spoke she was going through the trauma of separation. She was juggling a number of identities: being an American, living and working in Switzerland with children in English schools, and losing her identity as a wife. She was also the primary caregiver and breadwinner in the family as her husband had stopped working a few years before, suffering from depression. She described herself like 'a lost sheep that went adventuring a little bit too far' and was pining to 'go home to her tribe'. She had gone back to her university recently for a management course and when she went on campus, she had cried at the memory of having such a clear sense of belonging, such a singular identity when she had been there as a student. But now with children in the English school system, a job based in Switzerland and having effectively become a European, she described how her sense of belonging had become deeply eroded in the last few years. She talked about having to fashion a new identity around the constraint of being in London. Where previously she had been an ardent supporter and advocate for women's groups, which had provided her with her guiding purpose, she had become disillusioned by them, feeling that it was always women talking to women. She was now seeking 'some new endeavour that is more universal where men and women can talk collectively about things that matter to our common humanity'.

I'm conscious that Ellie's story encompasses more than just the challenge of reconciling competing identities at work because she is also dealing with losing her identity as a wife and shouldering the role of primary breadwinner and primary carer. So much is at sea for her that I think she is right in her quest to find a new endeavour to help guide her through these difficult times – something that is universal and transcends her day-to-day responsibilities. I believe that having such a guiding purpose often propels women through choppy waters and helps them to make choices about what to do, particularly when they lack sufficient women role models to consult or emulate.

When coaching women, I think it's imperative to focus on developing their purpose. Like identity, you don't find it, you develop it through trial and error and, as in Ellie's case, it might change with time. The coaching challenge is to help her figure out what motivates her, what she values and enjoys doing, and how this intersects with her skills and the job she's currently doing. A useful model for this is the Japanese concept of Ikigai shown in Figure 4.1.

When being interviewed for a podcast by Eleanor Mills, founder of an organisation devoted to mid-career women called Noon, CEO of WPP Karen Blackett succinctly articulated her own purpose: 'I see my purpose as giving opportunity to diverse talent' (Blackett and Mills, 2021).

As a Black woman leader who is also a mother, she must have faced myriad barriers, and right from the early days her own personal experiences helped shape the purpose that keeps her going. She makes the point that it's not just ethnicity and gender that are under-represented at senior levels in her industry,

Figure 4.1 The Ikigai diagram: a philosophical perspective

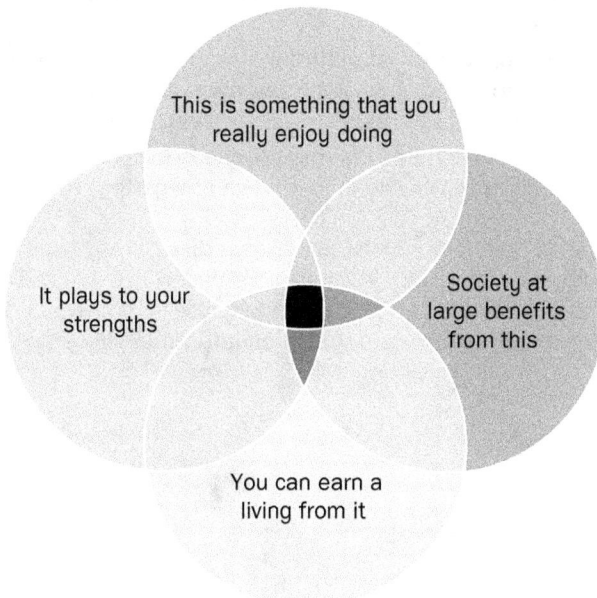

but highlights that 1 in 3 of the senior leaders in media are privately educated compared to 1 in 14 in the UK as a whole (Blackett and Mills, 2021).

You can see how Karen has found something that she's great at – presumably she loves doing it and gets paid for doing it. However, crucially, she uses her position to do something above and beyond her day job. She has introduced an array of initiatives that help her to fulfil her purpose of 'giving opportunity to diverse talent'.

Implications for coaching

Here is a summary of the key coaching points to take away from this chapter on identity and purpose:

- Understanding how one's leadership identity is formulated is critical in coaching women because the lack of suitable female role models can subtly put women off leadership.
- Encouraging women to act their way into leadership rather than thinking their way into it will forge their leadership identity.
- Having women appreciate that the prevailing style of leadership is changing will help encourage them to recognise their own leadership traits and not solely associate leadership with stereotypically masculine, agentic behaviours.
- Supporting women to merge their leadership identity with becoming a mother rather than choosing one over the other is vital for helping them avoid the 'mummy-track'.
- The VAST model provides a structure for supporting women through pregnancy and back to work, describing the transition in psychological terms and thereby normalising the experience for them.
- The Ikigai model is useful for having coachees focus on their guiding purpose because this acts as a North Star when navigating career transitions.

My experience of coaching women has shown that having clarity about one's identity and purpose helps build women's confidence. I've devoted the whole of the next chapter to the issue of confidence because it's so frequently described as a barrier to women's successful transition into leadership.

5 Confidence

I've chosen to dedicate a whole chapter to the issue of confidence, not just because it's so prevalent an issue when it comes to coaching but also because it's actually quite a complex picture. Nearly all of the women I have coached, and a significant number of men too, describe that they are lacking in confidence. They often report how they feel that they don't quite measure up, feel like they're a phony, have managed to pull the wool over people's eyes and are going to get found out. Here is Gail, 31, very successful in the macho world of tech investment, describing this feeling:

> I may have outward facing confidence, but I do have imposter syndrome ... When I first started in this role I felt almost like a con artist. I had massive imposter syndrome but then, you know, for the first six months I did feel out of my depth. I put loads of pressure on myself ... I questioned myself a lot and I got into having insomnia for about four months which was awful. And I think it all stemmed from all this pressure I was putting on myself to be good at my job. I don't think men, I mean some men have it, but I do feel that it's *very much* a trait that a woman would have versus a man. And even though I've got a great boss and I've had great feedback and amazing ratings the whole time I've been here, and I haven't really had any criticism, it's almost like I don't, I won't believe it.

Those women that I've coached that are further on in their career admit to still feeling it. What's interesting is that these feelings seem to transcend industry barriers. Gail works in the investment world, which is populated by men, but Debbie works in media, which has a far greater representation of women, albeit mainly at junior levels.

Debbie was appointed CEO of her agency a couple of years ago and says:

> You know it's funny, isn't it? You sort of think, 'Oh, now I'm in charge all those doubts will go away'. But they're just different things. Now it's do I come across with enough gravitas? Do I have influence? Am I demonstrating my position in the agency with clients? Am I too collaborative? That wrestle just continues. But, I am enjoying it a lot more. I have a lot more confidence in my values as Number One and know what I'm really good at – motivating teams and how I can, I suppose, persuade clients or how I deliver for my business.

There is evidence that women's confidence does increase with age. Research by Zenger and Folkman (2019) published in the *Harvard Business Review* indicates that this is the case. Zenger and Folkman collected data from more than

4,000 women and 3,000 men since 2016 and found about 30 per cent of women aged 25 or younger said they felt confident. About 50 per cent of men said the same. By age 40, women and men rate themselves equally confident. At age 60, women surpass men in confidence, on average. While men's confidence grows just 8.5 percentile points between ages 25 and 60+, women's confidence increases by 29 percentile points.

These findings tie in with Mainiero and Sullivan's Kaleidoscope Careers research previously described (2006). It points to women having a new lease of life when they get into the later stages of their careers, where they seek out work that chimes with their values and gives them more of a sense of purpose, which propels them towards feeling more at one with themselves. This manifests in greater levels of confidence.

Tackling imposter syndrome – some coaching techniques

It's worth looking at how the phenomenon of 'imposter syndrome' was first described. This notion was first developed by psychologists Pauline Rose Clance and Suzanne Imes (1978), who originally titled it 'imposter phenomenon' in their founding research on high-achieving women. They posited that 'despite outstanding academic and professional accomplishments, women who experience the imposter phenomenon persist in believing that they are really not bright and have fooled anyone who thinks otherwise'.

It's interesting to note how over time it morphed into being imposter 'syndrome', which makes it sound like a medical ailment. One of the principal ways that Clance and Imes (1978) suggested for tackling imposter phenomenon was therapy.

Some of the coaching techniques that can be deployed to help people experiencing a lapse in confidence are indeed drawn from those used in cognitive behavioural therapy.

- I introduce the concept of the 'inner critic' and normalise it by explaining that high performers, men or women, do tend to have a noisy inner critic. I encourage them to befriend their 'inner critic' because in a sense it's what's helped power their achievement drive. Visualising and bringing to life one's inner critic is helpful for minimising its impact. Somehow, giving it a name or even doing an illustration of it helps allay fear or shame and provides the opportunity to explore what might be old tapes that need updating in the light of experience.
- Another cognitive behavioural technique is to keep a 'thought record' when those feelings of inadequacy are most pronounced. Identifying triggers and interrupting the automatic response system where emotion takes over from thought is vital. This can be done by analysing the trigger event and subsequent feeling and then assigning supporting evidence and

contrary evidence to the strength of this feeling as a way of reducing its hold over you.

- Asking yourself how many times you have actually failed in a given situation and allowing your mind to entertain those times where you have felt the same level of fear but then gone on to be very successful works too. For some, it's helpful to draw attention to the link between imposter syndrome and extreme preparation. 'I only managed to carry it off because I was so well prepared' can become a self-defeating mantra that forces you into ever more preparation, some of which may be redundant. It's also not sustainable as you rise up and your role expands.

- I have some coachees practise prepping less. It feels counterintuitive but it's designed to help them believe that they know far more than they think they do and usually far more than anyone in the room. Sometimes bringing less data to the table can make you rely more on your wits and be more sensitive to the cues in the room rather than desperately rummaging through sheafs of paper you have brought with you and 'losing the room'. Often people use PowerPoint presentations as comfort blankets and can accidentally hide behind them rather than being more prepared to have a more interactive conversation.

- It's ironic that when you're feeling lacking in self-confidence you actually start to focus more on yourself rather than those around you. Coachees describe feeling 'huge in the room' as if everyone is focusing exclusively on them. I encourage them to instead notice what's going on around them, using mindful techniques such as asking yourself, 'What can you hear? What can you smell? What can you see?' In other words, I'm having them literally 'come to their senses'.

- Reframing being self-conscious as being self-oriented can work too, particularly for people who see themselves as very other-focused. The reality is when you are in a room with others, it's actually quite hard to gain and retain others' attention. We all over estimate how much attention is being paid to us.

- Positive affirmations can help to cut new neural pathways where you ask yourself last thing at night what three things you did well today and catch yourself obsessing about things you might have done wrong and metaphorically change the tape going around in your head.

- Focusing on strengths is critical. I'm always struck by how easily women can describe their weaknesses and by their genuine inability to come up with their strengths. Plenty of men also struggle with this but I definitely see a greater reluctance on the part of women to name their strengths, which is also manifest in a distaste for self-promotion which I'll return to later.

- When coaching women, it's useful to examine their speech patterns and identify what are known as 'tags', for example when you might end a statement with a question. There's evidence that this more querulous approach detracts from sounding confident. There is, however, equally sound evidence that women who do use this more interrogative language can be more influential. This relates to women having to sound more 'prosocial'. I'll expand on this later in this chapter. The whole subject of gender and language is much researched and Deborah Tannen (2013) and Robin T. Lakoff (1973) are good places to start. I take note of speech patterns, and I like to see how people express themselves on email too, but I'm not a big fan of changing up women's speech to make them 'sound' more confident. I prefer to work with women to have the confidence to be authentic. I always thought Margaret Thatcher sounded odd when she allegedly deliberately lowered her voice to make her come across more influentially.

Confidence is contextual

More than anything I like to reassure people that confidence is not an attribute and indeed imposter syndrome is not a disease or an ailment. Instead, both are states of mind and as such you can change them. Most people, when asked if they are a confident person, would answer, 'It depends'. This response reflects the highly contextual nature of confidence and segues nicely onto the issue of whether men are more confident than women. The narrative from some of the younger women I interviewed for this book seemed to point to the affirmative.

Ella, a consultant working for one of the Big 4 accountancy firms:

I think women doubt themselves more. Maybe that's me. I doubt myself a lot. And I compare myself with a lot of people around me and I don't know if boys do that as much.

Caroline, a recruitment consultant:

I think guys are a bit more carefree. And potentially, I don't know whether it's just that they don't voice their anxieties but they still have them? They just don't voice them in the same way that women do. I don't think they don't necessarily feel them, but they definitely wouldn't portray them in the same way or vocalise them.

I was struck by how two of my older coachees instantly responded to my question about why they thought there were too few female leaders with the answer that it was all about confidence.

Here is Jane, a senior partner in a law firm sharing her experience of why there are still fewer women partners:

Definitely confidence. I think a lot of women still think the man could probably do it better if I'm honest. They (the young women associates) are much more shy and not assertive enough in meetings and just let points go ... they view it as a quality that they are quite measured. So they don't actually put themselves forward.

From Ted, a senior banker I've coached in the past and known a long time:

> *I don't see people as male or female at things, right, but what I do see from females is that it's almost as if they lack confidence, right?*

I think Ted is right to be querulous. His question, '*It's almost as if they lack confidence?*' is worth examining more closely.

Looking at the issue of confidence through a different lens

Maybe the problem isn't that women lack confidence but that confidence in women is not rewarded in the work world? If confidence is contextual, then perhaps women subconsciously know that there's a penalty to being perceived as over-confident and moderate their behaviours accordingly.

Vicky, one of my younger interviewees, seemed prepared to challenge the prevailing orthodoxy. When I asked her about confidence and women, she had a different take on things. On the idea that women lack confidence:

> [This] *frustrates me a lot. I wonder if that's a bit outdated to be honest because I look around and it doesn't resonate with anyone I know. I look around at my friends, my female colleagues and think, 'Yeah, you're a bunch of unconfident women who are afraid to put yourself out there?' (The implicit response was 'No way!'). And so, I don't actually think it's an issue of female confidence, I think it's an issue with how people react to female confidence. And I do wonder if it's an easy get out for why women are not getting promoted. 'Oh, it's because they're not asking for it and that's women's faults because they're not confident' ... Could it actually be that, not just men but HR professionals too and businesses, are looking for a reason why so few women are promoted and they just ascribe it to confidence? I don't like the narrative that women aren't confident, and I don't think it's true. And I think you're in danger of making it worse by continuing that narrative.*

A very different response to the norm and one that has sound research backing, as I'll go on to explain.

We have come a long way since 2014 when Sheryl Sandberg encouraged women to 'lean in' in her famous Ted Talk and subsequent book. Her message at that time was later deemed to be a bit 'fix the women' and not enough 'fix the system' in its prevailing narrative. A piece of research carried out by Guillén et al., written up in a *Forbes India* article in 2017, entitled 'For Women, self-confidence not enough for workplace success', reflects an angle much more in line with Vicky's perception.

This study was of 4,000 people from a global software company, and it looked at supervisors' 'perceptions of how confident their employees appear to be in their ability to successfully complete their job responsibilities'. It concluded that if you do your job well, then you will be perceived as confident whether you're a man or a woman, which I think makes sense. Being competent can equate to being perceived as confident. But what was interesting was that when high-performing men appear self-confident, this allowed them to be influential in the organisation, but this was only true for women who are described as 'prosocial', in other words, nice people. For high-performing women to be influential they also had to be seen to conform to stereotypical feminine traits, such as being warm and caring – hence the subtle pressure to end statements with a question as mentioned earlier. So, the takeaway for men is 'as long as you can get stuff done, you'll be influential', but its conclusion for women is more along the lines of 'If you want to be influential and thus be able to progress, make sure you perform and also invest time in helping others and being a good citizen'. The research also emphasised how twice as much prosocial language is used in performance reviews for women than for men. Again, we're coming up against the double-bind dilemma outlined in Chapter 3, where it's important to be aware that there are different standards being applied to women than men.

So how does this play out in practice?

I think Suzy from chapter 3 describes well the draining effect of trying to influence in her previous ad agency, where she felt the prevailing culture was very macho and she was given feedback to the effect that she could be more confident.

> You're just put in these rooms with these men who, quite frankly, I don't think valued my opinion anyway. And then you're expected to peacock. It was almost, 'Show me how good you are'. It was as though they couldn't see what I'd delivered, the output of my work. I was definitely encouraged to have more of a voice and there's a temptation to do it in a certain way. And I had to sort of wrestle with that, I suppose. Because part of the time I knew that the only way to succeed was to play their game … and I guess that's quite draining isn't it afterwards because you're playing two games there? You're not just playing with one hand of cards as a lot of them are.

Suzy didn't feel that she could actually say that she didn't want to play their game, which to her mind was about peacocking and power games which she really wasn't either interested in or equipped to play.

Another telling anecdote about the strongly gendered nature of the association of confidence with success can be seen in Jane's, the senior lawyer referenced before, comments about women:

> I did notice, which is a bit of a funny thing, that I also think that women with a deeper voice get on better. And I've come across in my career women who were very intelligent but spoke with very high voices and it really did them no favours.

When I queried why that might be:

> Because it didn't equate to them being taken seriously and it's completely
> unfair and completely irrational. The woman I'm thinking about always wore
> lots of jewellery and when she walked around the office, you could hear her
> jingle. And, you know, that did her no favours either but what can you do? You
> can't tell a woman in her 40s to start dressing differently. But she never made
> it to equity partner.

In Jane's comments you can hear the contradiction of, on the one hand thinking
it's irrational to judge people by the fact they are essentially being more
'feminine', but also her perception that the resolution to the problem was that
someone tell her to stop dressing like a woman, in other words 'fix the woman'.
Jane, herself an equity partner, seemed to agree that dressing in too feminine a
way distracted from being taken seriously.

So again, when it comes to confidence it's so important to highlight systemic
bias for the women you're coaching, as you cannot assume that women will see
it, even if they have been a casualty of it.

Damned if you do, damned if you don't

I once coached a Russian woman banker who was irritated by not always being
taken seriously by her male colleagues and sometimes even by the companies
coming in to pitch for loans. She definitely wasn't conforming to the 'dress like
a man' unwritten rule. She had dyed her hair very blonde and wore tight white
dresses and high shoes and always had the latest in designer handbags. She
confided that she received quite a lot of critical feedback about her appear-
ance, but she had worked out her coping mechanism. She said that when it was
assumed in any given meeting that she was the secretary or there to make the
tea, which happened a lot, she would point out that she had a double first in
maths and she wouldn't be making the tea. Indeed, she would be making the
decision as to whether they would be investing in **them**.

She rather relished turning the tables in this way and enjoyed seeing the
surprise on their faces. However, the result was that she not only got feedback about dressing 'like a prostitute' from her colleagues, was on the
receiving end of innumerable innuendos about 'what exactly was her relationship' with certain male clients, but she also got feedback for being 'too
bolshie'! You have to have a lot of self-confidence in the face of that kind of
feedback.

Much of her confidence came from having a mother who had always worked
as a professor and also having been brought up in Russia, where she experienced less sexism against women with jobs. For her, the woman as the caregiver
was a very pernicious stereotype here in the UK.

When we discussed the impressions she created, I couldn't help admiring her
steadfast defence of her right to dress in flattering clothes and display her

hard-earned wealth with the expensive handbags and shoes. She was determined not to be cowed by what she saw as English people's snobbishness about Russian conspicuous wealth. She was going to do it her way irrespective of others' biased judgements.

I met her some time later and was disappointed to see that the dyed hair had gone and the white dress and high heels. I guess she felt she had to conform after all and I got the impression her determination had gradually been whittled away. It made me sad.

I tell this story because it's an indication of the dance women have to perform to be taken seriously and also it points to the challenge of trying to stay true to yourself. Women 'might be told confidence is the key to professional success, that's rarely the case in practice. Unless women can temper their assertiveness with more stereotypically feminine traits like empathy and altruism, confidence will do little to advance their careers' (Mahoney, 2019). My Russian banker was pushing back against two stereotypes. It seemed to me that she was condemned for dressing too much like a woman and acting too much like a man.

Confidence and self-promotion

Finally, I come to the issue of why women appear to be reluctant to self-promote. Confidence is often conflated with self-promotion. These are entirely different. Confidence is a state of mind, a feeling, and self-promotion is a behaviour. Even highly confident women do not like to self-promote because they fear the backlash for doing so. A fascinating piece of research in the NBER by Exley and Kesler carried out at the end of 2019 showed quite conclusively that women will consistently underscore themselves compared to men, particularly on what are perceived to be male-type tests, in this case a maths and science test. What was particularly noteworthy was that even when they were told that they had performed well in the test, when it came to questions about whether they would put themselves forward for a job that required these skills they had just been tested on, they still marked themselves less suitable than their male counterparts.

However, rather than focus on confidence boosting strategies, I completely concur with the author of that report's suggestion that it might be wise to 'de-emphasise subjective evaluations relative to more objective metrics to determine hiring and promotion decisions or investigative strategies to change perceptions of gender norms or the norms themselves' (Exley and Kesler, 2019: 4).

Surely we need to be turning to men and advocating that they no longer place so much importance on self-promotion as a key leadership skill when it's now posited that self-awareness, self-regulation, authenticity and humility are more called-for traits in today's world? We need leaders to accustom themselves to focus more on deliverables than the ability to sell oneself. We also need leaders to demonstrate sufficient empathy to recognise the difference between self-esteem and projected self-confidence, something which is groomed in men from a young age and frowned upon in women.

Last word on confidence

So, in conclusion, as a coach it's vital to have all of the techniques in your tool-kit for addressing confidence lapses but it's equally important to draw attention to the wider context in which they are operating. As Jessica Valenti (2014) said in an article about the books *Lean In* (Sandberg, 2015) and *The Confidence Code* (Kay and Shipman, 2014), 'You can't self-help away deeply ingrained structural discrimination'. Coaching women to handle imposter phenomenon will only go so far, instead I feel there's more merit in coaching them to call out bias and push for performance appraisals that rely less on self-evaluation, lest they fall victim to men's tendency to score themselves higher than women. This is very fertile ground for coaching women to fix the system rather than fix themselves.

Part 2

6 Coaching with an agenda

In Part Two of the book, I invite you to stand back and consider coaching women in a wider context. I will focus on the systemic influences on women's careers, looking at where coaching can have an impact at a macro level to help smooth women's path into leadership.

But first, in this chapter I want to return to the question of whether as a coach we can ever be fully impartial. I will first cover the importance of distinguishing between your own agenda and others' agendas. I run through the origin of person-centred coaching and show how this ethos has understandably permeated the coaching profession. I then challenge the notion of whether it's possible, or even desirable, in some instances to leave your agenda at the door. This is followed by a look at the issue of how we address difference in the room with a specific intersectional focus. Lastly, this brings me onto how much of oneself one could bring into the coaching space in an attempt at making it a safe space for coachees while still respecting the principle of client-focused coaching.

Back in 1994 when I first started out as a professional coach, as I have already explained, the profession was very much still in its infancy. It has changed dramatically since then with multiple coaching bodies emerging, such as ICF, EMCC, AOEC and the AC to name just a few, who are attempting to provide some form of consistency and regulation.

Irrespective of the coaching body with which you are affiliated, coaches all owe much to the influence of Carl Rogers, the originator of a person-centred approach to humanistic psychology back in the 1950s. His approach signalled a significant change in the power dynamic between therapist and patient. Rogerian theory requires that the therapist listen with acceptance and without judgement, to facilitate change in their client. This was quite a departure from the expert/patient dynamic that existed at the time. It is premised on the belief that individuals have agency and full potential and the therapist's role is to release this potential by the skilful use of non-judgemental questions and by holding their client in unconditional positive regard. Coaches reading this will no doubt recognise these basic tenets as part of their own coaching practice.

EISPU model

This model of communication, which underpins Rogers' person-centred approach, is very instructive for coaches as it considers the different responses available to us when someone opens a conversation (unfortunately, the original source is no longer available, but changingminds.org sums it up succinctly). It categorises the responses into five types and offers a ranking in terms of prevalence of usage:

Evaluative – most common; prone to being judgemental
Interpretive – second-most common; making assumptions and jumping to conclusions
Supportive – third-most common; offering agreement
Probing – second-least common; asking open-ended questions
Understanding – least common; behaving in a non-evaluative way.

To bring this to life I've included a conversation between two fictional characters, Jane and Alison:

Jane – 'I've been in this job for seven years now.'
Alison – 'I once stayed in a job too long as well. You really need to move on.'

This is an example of an **evaluative** response where Alison automatically moves into advice mode with a declarative statement.
 A variation on this might be an **interpretive** statement:

Jane – 'I've been in this job for seven years now.'
Alison – 'Yes, you must be bored with it by now.'

A significant proportion of human conversation takes this form where we make assumptions about what's meant by someone's initial gambit, usually based on our own experience.
 Less prevalent in every day conversation are **supportive** statements such as:

Alison – 'Really? Seven years.'

Notice this is merely a repeat of what's been said, giving Jane the chance to hear how it sounds.
 Even less common, according to the research, are responses which reveal a true curiosity, using **probing** to facilitate self-exploration.

Alison – 'How are you feeling about that?'

Here she's using an open-ended question to draw Jane out.
 Another interaction, which doesn't happen as often as you might imagine in common parlance, is one where Alison might show she's listened and really understood what's behind Jane's statement. This is an **understanding** response. Often this might just be silence, a much under-utilised response, which has the benefit of giving Jane time to think. Nancy Kline's (2002) seminal work *Time to*

Think expands on the value of silence in coaching and she offers multiple examples of how, by saying nothing or by simply asking, 'What else?' coachees often gravitate to the real issue they're facing as the time to think has allowed them the chance to analyse what's really going on for them. This is often so much more valuable than having someone immediately jumping in to rescue them.

The point about the example is that we can't be sure from Jane's initial statement what's behind what was meant without exploring further. Jane could have been expressing pride at her staying power. She could have been expressing dissatisfaction with being there too long, or maybe Jane is merely musing with a thought that's just popped into her head! Of course, it's a rather fatuous example as it depends entirely on how well-acquainted Jane and Alison are, because the closer you are the more likely you're going to get your interpretations correct. We also can't hear the tone or see the whole person, which is often far more instructive than the words themselves. But it does serve to illustrate the point about how quickly most people move into advice mode, believing that is what is wanted of them.

How many times have you found yourself on the receiving end of well-meaning advice from friends and family when all you really wanted was to be listened to and feel understood? It's as though we are hard wired to proffer solutions when we become aware of someone's expressed discomfort. We feel moved to act to reduce the tension and clarify the confusion. However, it's worth bearing in mind that when someone brings to you what they feel to be an intractable problem it's actually quite insulting to have them imagine you have solved it in minutes! It's important to pay due deference to the emotion it's evoking in the person and be curious in order to help them explore what it's bringing up in them. Moving into the probing and understanding parts of the model and becoming skilled with the various techniques is part and parcel of learning to be a good coach.

Getting off your own agenda

When it comes to learning to coach, an essential precept is to have trainees practise probing and understanding and to get off their own agenda. The early part of our Professional Coach Recognition Programme, where we train coaches, is very much focused on practising the skill of asking questions and listening without an agenda. In workshops we have participants come up with a topic they feel particularly strongly about without revealing what their views are. We then find someone who has (or is prepared to take) an opposing view. We pair them up, provide them with an observer to follow the process and set the challenge for the person with the strong view to ask open-ended questions that do not reveal their hand. If, and more likely, when, the questioner does ask a loaded question, the observer intervenes.

It's harder than it sounds. So, for example, if I believed that everyone should have a Covid vaccine passport, the challenge for me would be to see how many open-ended questions I could ask my partner about the topic without revealing my hand. Questions like 'Can you see how it would make going to events safer if we all had a passport?' would obviously miss the mark, whereas 'What's your view on Covid passports?' and 'Tell me what you think about the possible introduction of Covid passports,' would be allowed. I think of this as using 'clean' questions, ones where there is no expressed agenda. (There's a plethora of literature on this topic and I believe it's essential reading for new coaches.)

It's worth giving this a go yourself … Try remaining in questioning mode without revealing your view next time a heated discussion is brewing and notice how much more easily and fully the other person expresses their viewpoint rather than automatically countering yours or perhaps just giving in to you. You will find it is so much more constructive as it defuses conflict.

As a coach this is an elementary part of the coaching training. I'm completely on board with Carl Roger's belief that if you hold back and trust that the other person has the capacity to reach their own conclusions then better outcomes can often result. Sometimes you might not understand how they've reached that conclusion, but that's ok.

I like to start my coaching sessions by checking what my coachee's 'take outs' were from the previous session. I'm still occasionally chastened by the realisation that what seemed **to me** to have been an 'aha' for them, can go completely unnoticed by my coachee. Coaching is a humble profession and feeling completely cool about this is very important. If you find yourself as a coach wanting to 'remind' them what they got out of the session you haven't yet clocked that another person's mental landscape is new territory and probably does not resemble yours at all. Your version of an 'aha' will almost certainly be different from theirs. Your role is to help **them** have 'ahas' and if you find yourself having them for your coachee, you're interpreting and not probing and understanding.

Seeing the coaching partnership as a journey of discovery is a helpful analogy even if the expression itself is a tad clichéd. As my intention is to understand, I find that I'm mostly listening in the first few coaching sessions as I get to know someone and enter their mental landscape. Being comfortable with ambiguity helps me because if my focus is on achieving absolute clarity, I might ask too many questions and interrupt my coachee's flow. Mainly I try to stay out of judgement and stick to listening attentively to their story while being observant about how they tell their story. I find my 'P', preference for perceiving over 'J' for judging in Myers Briggs terms, i.e. my comfort with going with the flow rather than a need for structure and clarity is helpful when it comes to allowing my client free rein. In this respect, I'm acting on my training, which is to quieten my influence in the conversation to ensure my coachee has space to think and to take it in the direction that they want it to go.

Having just emphasised the importance of staying off one's agenda, I have increasingly been questioning this and asking myself if I perhaps overdo my determination to stay off my agenda and whether I could, perhaps even should, introduce more of me into the coaching space.

What if you do have an agenda?

This brings me to a new framework for coaching that's emerging – the idea of New Generation coaching as described by Hettie Einzig in her excellent book *The Future of Coaching* (2017). As Einzig puts it, to stay off our agenda:

> demands of us a choice: denial or engagement with the world; either way to pretend to cling to neutrality is disingenuous, bordering on bad faith. Whether leader or coach it behooves us to choose our values and our position towards the world, our work and our purpose. (p. 49)

I first came upon Hettie Einzig at a coaching conference dedicated to looking at how coaches can influence the world with respect to ensuring a more sustainable future. A big topic, to be sure. It was in this context that her challenge really made me stop and think.

How do we square our belief in the power of the individual with our own strong sense of what needs to happen in the world? Given my strong belief in the need for the world to have a more diverse set of people making the decisions, how can I coach without explicitly sharing that agenda? So much of the coach training focuses on remaining impartial that at times this may be in conflict with the need to be authentic when in the coaching space. This has given me much pause for thought over the years.

My colleague and fellow coach Aboodi Shabi goes further and challenges the coaching profession to ask itself what its purpose is. In an interview on LinkedIn with Lydia Stevens (Shabi and Stevens, 2021) he argues that 'when coaching, you cannot just be a bystander saying, "Tell me what you want and let me help you get there." We have to stand for something'. While he urges us to consider the deep philosophical issues facing us today, such as climate change and diversity, equity and inclusion he also recommends humility too. 'We need to hold ourselves lightly and be able to laugh at ourselves.' I interpret this as seeing our input in the great scheme of life in perspective. He sums it up nicely by saying, 'We're just here to have conversations with people to help them figure out what life is about.'

I like that definition of coaching and, although I certainly bring an ethos of non-directivity into my coaching, I can see that they are not mutually exclusive and indeed it's a more honest relationship if you bring more of yourself into the coaching relationship. What this brings to the fore for me is the importance of really understanding what you believe in before you embark on helping others. I really believe in a fairer world for all, and my focus is on helping to make companies more diverse. This has found its expression in gender diversity. However, I don't think you can consider inequity in the system without also considering race. If you believe in equality for women, I feel you must recognise intersectionality. In other words, recognise that we do not all experience discrimination to the same extent.

Knowing your values is one thing, but knowing your scope is another. I know that I'm still learning when it comes to knowing how best to address intersectionality in the work I do with women. I'm hovering between conscious incompetence and conscious competence. I suspect, as someone who benefits from white privilege, I may never fully get to unconscious competence. However, I do think it's important to keep trying and to reflect critically on experience, rather than give up in the face of the fear of getting it wrong.

Unconscious bias on my part

To illustrate with an example, can I now draw you back to Chapter 2 where I introduced you to Anita? I have altered the names of all the women that I write about in the book, but in this particular case I deliberately chose a Western-sounding name even though Anita is of Indian heritage. I now want you to consider her story again in the light of this knowledge. Does it make you see things any differently?

As an Asian woman, albeit with a very Western education and upbringing, I surmised that there might be different expectations on Anita based on her culture. There were times in our coaching conversations where I suppressed some of my questions about the division of labour in Anita's household. I've since had cause to question my own reticence on this issue. Did I challenge her enough in that opening session where I usually pursue the concept of conscious co-parenting? Did I pull my punches with Anita due to some inbuilt perception I had about the expectations on her because she is Asian? In retrospect, I can see that I was feeling that the division of labour was 'unfair', and I think I did check myself from being more challenging. I worried about letting my own Western Feminist perspective leak into the conversation. In this way I was suppressing my 'agenda' in the sense of being non-directive, but was I being authentic? Why didn't I admit that's what I was feeling? I did perceive a difference and yet I didn't draw attention to it. That brings me to the question: To what extent should we bring our difference more pointedly into our contracting conversations?

Addressing difference head-on

I'm very taken by the work of Carol Campayne and her company the Diversity Practice. She talks on her website about maximising difference rather than minimising it because in doing that you can 'bridge boundaries and shift mindsets'. After attending one of her workshops, my team and I had a follow-up meeting with her team to learn more about their mission to help clients 'work positively with the dynamics of difference'. I was keen to know how I introduce difference in the coaching space and her advice was simple but powerful. She suggested asking, 'How can our difference be of service in the coaching?' in contracting conversations.

So, I decided to go back to a few women of colour that I had coached recently for their thoughts on how/whether I could have pointed more to our differences at the outset of our coaching sessions. Their responses gave me good food for thought.

- **Maria** felt that it would be a good 'open-ended way to start the conversation' and that drawing on a different perspective would be a good thing as she appreciated another lens through which to look at things.
- **Eleana**, herself a clinical psychologist, would have been tempted to turn the question back to me and ask, 'In what way do **you** think our difference would be helpful?' I realised I wasn't sure how I would answer it, which was noteworthy. How did I expect her to answer it?
- **Julie** said she would have 'politely declined to discuss race and ethnicity' and wasn't drawn to the question at all because she was far more interested in what united us as women and not what separated us, i.e. colour.

What they did all agree was the importance of introducing my identity upfront. So, in other words, what might be a good way to open the conversation would be to describe my identity as a white, female, Scottish, mother, wife, coach and leader in my sixties. Only through bringing myself fully into the room and offering more of myself am I generating the right circumstances in which a question such as Carol's might land well.

I think rather than simply noting what they agreed, however, it is more pertinent to draw attention to how different their responses were. But of course, they were! Because it was a reflection of their unique personalities and experiences in all their richness. It's a very good reminder of why the expression 'BAME women' is so alienating for women of colour. It is a form of stereotyping, lumping people together and overlooking the essential uniqueness of human beings. In fact, my seeking out only 'women of colour' to enquire about this could be perceived in itself as a form of 'othering' where you make people feel they do not belong.

So, what is my takeout from this experience? I think it is that although I see the value in Carol's question, it is only by creating the necessary psychological safety quickly in the room that my coachee will open up. I will return to how one creates that psychological safety in Chapter 9 when I explore inclusive leadership. I must anticipate, however, that some, like Julie, might politely decline to discuss race and ethnicity and instead focus on what unites us. And of course, I've recognised that this is a question that's worth asking in all my contracting sessions and not simply those where I see a difference with my eyes.

Introducing your agenda when coaching leaders

When it comes to coaching all leaders, I can see that I need to bring more of myself into the chemistry sessions when they are deciding whether to work with me. I have started to introduce my belief in inclusive leadership into my chemistry check conversation to give a sense of where I stand on the issue of leadership. I talk a bit about how it's key for leaders to be inclusive given the increasingly global and diverse world in which we live. In this way I'm engaging them in a conversation that allows them a keener understanding of my perspective, my filter on the world. I'm at pains to point out that I don't feel I have a monopoly on leadership thinking and that not everyone might see it in the same vein. I don't have the answers, but rather I can provide a setting that is conducive to finding the answers to increasingly complex questions or perhaps just formulating the right questions to be asking.

So much of leadership is about addressing paradoxes and balancing competing priorities that I see my role as being a thinking partner in facing those challenges. In this respect, I understand the importance of not being overly attached to my own theories. I invite prospective coachees to share their vision of leadership and in doing so I'm hopefully demonstrating that the dynamic I'm hoping to create is one of sharing and challenging.

I have also found it useful to send a relevant article or video to help expand on my definition of good leadership as a follow-up. In this way I'm letting the prospective coachee know what I stand for. When you think about it, it's only fair that you level with the person for whom you are going to be a thinking partner about your own belief system. Of course, you have to get the balance right because you are also demonstrating your questioning approach, and so a long diatribe about your beliefs would be a turn-off.

On reflection, I wonder if in the past I have perhaps erred too much on the side of going into sponge mode? Perhaps I've been going into coach mode too early, imagining that I'm demonstrating my value through the power of my questions? I'm currently experimenting with taking the time to give a better account of myself, or better put, to give more of myself when I first meet them, to allow prospective coachees to have a sense of my identity as my coachees had advised me.

Introducing your agenda when coaching mothers

Because we do so much work in this area, I've been considering how my agenda differs when I'm doing Parental Transition Coaching. My overall purpose remains the same. I want to help create a world where there are more diverse teams led by inclusive leaders. This works when coaching all parents, but I do get more specific with women by saying that I believe that a woman can be a mother and still have a vibrant career and therefore that it's my hope that the coaching will help her navigate the road ahead. I also share with her that I personally have a strong investment in seeing more women become leaders because I think society would benefit from more women being central to decision-making that affects us all.

As the women I coach are always in professional jobs in corporate settings and the coaching is paid for by the organisation, it's also incumbent upon me to explain that I'm acting on behalf of the client company. I make it clear that by engaging me, the company is hoping that the coaching will help to retain her. However, and this is crucial, I'm also clear that she is my client in this relationship and that the confidentiality contract is definitely between us and so she can feel free to explore all her options. It's a legitimate choice to leave corporate life or a specific company when becoming a mother and it's not my role to dissuade them but it is my role to broaden out the discussion and to perhaps help them understand what's behind their decision, bearing in mind the gendered script that's playing out around them. They could have a burning desire to set up their own company, or they could want to take full advantage of the time to be with their new-born, it doesn't matter. My role is not to judge or persuade despite my over-riding desire to see more women in leadership. The fact that a number of women who did choose to leave their organisation have remained in touch is, I hope, testament to my ability to stay objective.

I do not give feedback directly to the client. Where we are coaching 'en masse' in an organisation, our coaches share themes about what's going on for parents going through the parental transition. Those themes have proven invaluable in fleshing out my own experiences when coaching. The sole purpose of feeding back these themes to our clients is to help them consider more ways to support parents at this key juncture. By assuring confidentiality, I'm helping to create that psychologically safe space for those I coach to explore all options during the coaching process, including leaving the organisation. Getting the balance right between my purpose and the company's desire to retain talented women, with my coachee's need to be understood and accepted on their terms, can be tricky and requires careful consideration and understanding of the differing agendas in the room, and clear contracting is an important prerequisite.

Bringing more of yourself into coaching

On the issue of how to bring more of yourself into the room, a related question is: 'To what extent should I bring in my own lived experience into a coaching session?' I'm so wary of 'leading the witness' that my inclination has been to steer clear of sharing my own experiences. However, an occasion a number of years ago made me think twice about that inclination. A woman leader I was coaching had experienced a very traumatic event in her personal life. She didn't initially reveal this to me as it was something about which she had deep feelings of shame. She only felt comfortable volunteering it after I, intuitively sensing that she wasn't completely trusting me and was holding back, decided to reveal something very personal from my own background, which revealed my vulnerability. It wasn't planned, it somehow just felt right at the time. At the end of the coaching engagement, she said that my decision to reveal more of myself had been the turning point in our coaching relationship. I too felt the palpable difference that this personal disclosure created between us.

I brought this to my supervision session where my supervisor helpfully suggested that the question to ask myself when considering whether to introduce my experience is 'To what extent is my sharing this experience in service of my client's agenda?' Intuitively I had felt that on this occasion it was in service of the coaching. I had spontaneously confided something personal in her and it turned out to have been a turning point in the coaching for her. Openness can beget openness and showing my own vulnerability clearly made her feel safer confiding in me.

Like many of my clients, I don't find it easy to share my insecurities. I was brought up by parents who used humour to handle difficult emotion and considered discussing insecurities as weakness. I was then schooled in the rational, predominantly male, managerial world where vulnerability still struggles to rear its head. It's interesting to reflect that although in the past I may not have always consciously shared my experience, I was still revealing myself. I was leaking a 'be strong' mantra. Let me explain.

Around the same time as I realised how impactful my sharing something vulnerable had been with my coachee, I had another insight from a leader I was coaching. He asked to postpone our next coaching session until he was feeling better about himself. When I queried this, he said that he liked to feel he was on top of his game when he came to see me, otherwise it would be a waste of a session. You can imagine the richness of the conversation that I had in my supervision session following that comment.

What was I signalling that made him feel that he needed to be on form to get the most out of our sessions? Was I conveying too much of a focus on 'onwards and upwards' and rushing into action planning? Perhaps I wasn't spending enough time in probing mode? What was it about my own energy that might not be giving people licence to feel flat when they're with me? Was I inadvertently perpetuating the always-on, high-performance culture of the environment he was in rather than providing a safe space for him to be able to have a 'shoes off' conversation? Was I channelling my parents and conveying that I thought it a weakness to discuss insecurities?

These two pieces of feedback had a big impact on me. Around that time, I decided to embark on some therapy to better understand myself. Through this I became acquainted with the work of Irving Yalom, which stopped me in my tracks and really changed the way I think about the dynamic between myself and my coachees. It got me thinking much more richly about how much of ourselves we bring into every relationship whether we intend to or not.

I learned a lot about myself in those sessions; for example, I crystallised my tendency to describe things in quite binary terms despite intellectually being able to embrace a much more nuanced understanding of an issue. I noticed a real tension in my desire to move things on but at the same time understand things in depth. These insights have really helped me develop, but the issue that I found most revealing was around my discomfort with vulnerability. This led me to the realisation that I may well be unintentionally signalling that it wasn't ok to be vulnerable around me. It seemed perhaps I was channelling my parents.

Further training with my friend and fellow coach Roxanne Hobbs led me to Brené Brown and her work on vulnerability (2010). From that I learned that to be empathic one must first embrace one's own vulnerability and this is something that I continue to work on. Deepening my self-understanding and emotional regulation is key for both my development as a coach and a leader to enable me to support others. Understanding what triggers my threat system allows me to come to my coaching interactions much better prepared for the job of assisting others to make sense of their own reactions in an increasingly challenging world. I will return to this in Chapter 9 when I explain more about leading inclusively.

A simple tool for introducing the emotional realm into coaching is called the Emotional Barometer (EB) (see Figure 6.1). I learned about it from Dr Brian Marien (2018). Brian is Founder and Director of the Positive Group, a company dedicated to improving the psychological wellbeing, resilience and performance of individuals. Brian and his team provided some really excellent training for myself and my coach team at ECC on the neuroscience of coaching and the EB was one of my key takeouts.

There is an app where you can plot your moods and your team's moods and analyse this over time, an exercise I found very revealing. Tracking this helped me realise what caused me to be in different quadrants and to understand and better regulate my emotions. I've drastically simplified the tool and I draw it quickly at the beginning of coaching sessions to ask my coachee where they would plot themselves right now. The graph is empty so they can use their own words. I have simply populated this version with typical descriptors. I feel that this conveys that it's ok and quite normal to be at different parts of the graph.

Figure 6.1 The emotional barometer

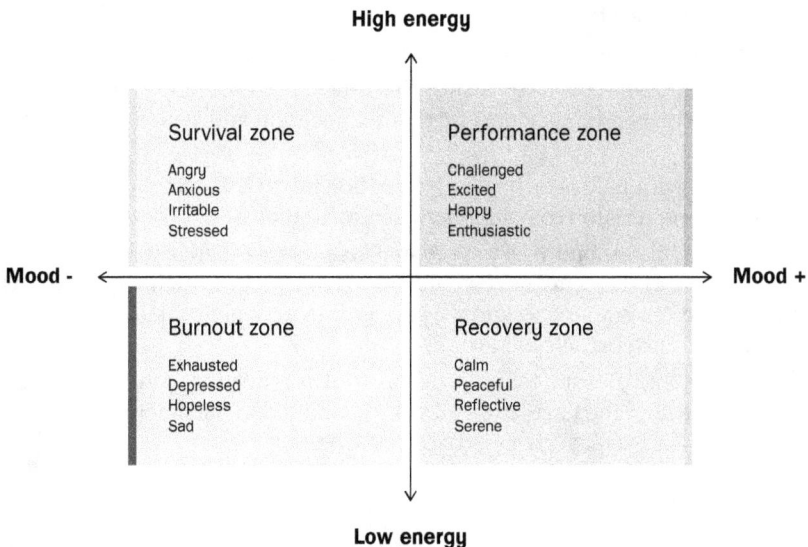

High energy

Survival zone	Performance zone
Angry	Challenged
Anxious	Excited
Irritable	Happy
Stressed	Enthusiastic

Mood -   Mood +

Burnout zone	Recovery zone
Exhausted	Calm
Depressed	Peaceful
Hopeless	Reflective
Sad	Serene

Low energy

Everyone is subject to mood swings and our energy waxes and wanes dramatically too. I feel by drawing attention to this I am signalling that it is indeed OK to not feel on top form all the time.

I can see now that I may have been assuming that I always had to be in the top right corner and so my 'professional front', i.e. bright and breezy, was rubbing off on my clients. I think I had conflated being professional with being upbeat. My own 'be strong' mantra had crept into my coaching and manifested itself in an inclination to ask questions to elicit the positives and move people to action. I believe that I am now better at being with someone irrespective of where they are on the Emotional Barometer.

I now temper my undoubted preference for galvanising action with a greater understanding of the value of staying with negative emotion and being more comfortable and, indeed, more vulnerable in this space. There's much to be learned from life's lows and I'm pleased to note that I've found my clients to be considerably more likely to reach out when they're feeling down since having that realisation.

Implications for coaching

To conclude, here is a summary of the coaching takeouts from this chapter:

- Being able to ask 'clean' open-ended questions rather than leading questions is step one in being a good coach.
- Giving a good account of yourself, your purpose and your agenda is helpful in the chemistry session to enable your coachee to appreciate that it's a coaching partnership and that your purpose is beyond acting as a mirror to reflect back their thoughts.
- Being alert to your own unconscious biases requires ongoing vigilance.
- Enquiring about how discussing differences in coaching could help the coaching partnership is worth further exploration and sensitive experimentation.
- Working on yourself is critical to ensure you have dealt with your own 'stuff' to better prepare you to help others deal with theirs.
- Coachees will respond well to personal disclosure on your part as long as it is in service of the coachee. I would advise using it sparingly if you're a new coach. It takes practice to know when your experience is relevant – most of the time it clutters their picture.
- The Emotional Barometer is a useful tool for helping you to meet your coachees where they are, from an energy and mood perspective.

7   Coaching in the system

As the basic premise of the book is that we must not fix the women, we must fix the system, I have devoted this chapter to defining the system that this refers to and examining different participants' parts in upholding it. I use the term 'broken bridge' as a metaphor for women's relationship to the system. I end by describing how coaches can influence the system using the ECC Six Stages of a Woman's Career model (ECC, n.d.) to highlight that those interventions change depending on where women are in their career.

What is the system?

When you think about a system what perhaps comes to mind is a computer system, a biological system like the muscular system, or maybe a political system. When I talked to the managing partner at a large US law firm about a women's leadership programme, I mentioned in passing the need to fix the system and not the women. His reaction was, 'What system? It sounds like you're describing a 1950s communist state.' He had no concept of the system I was referring to and I found myself struggling to convey to him what it meant.

It put me in mind of David Foster Wallace's famous commencement speech at Kenyon College:

> There are these two young fish swimming along and they happen to meet an older fish swimming the other way, who nods at them and says, 'Morning boys. How's the water?' And the two young fish swim on for a bit, and then eventually one of them looks over at the other and goes 'What the hell is water?' (Wallace, 2005)

When I was met by the challenge 'What system?' I felt like the older fish in the fish tank. For me, the system is everywhere, it's what we live and breathe, and it regulates the world in which we live. The system is the social, political and organisational context in which we exist. For me, thinking systemically is the way to frame and navigate the complexity of the world we inhabit. There are systems within systems and the particular system that I had assumed we were discussing when considering why so few women were making it to partner was a system that favoured men. I was thinking about the patriarchy. I find myself frequently unwilling to name it for fear of provoking scorn or outright derision. A definition of the patriarchy is:

> *A system of society or government in which men hold the power and women are largely excluded from it.* (Oxford Dictionary)

I recognise that many of you reading this might not subscribe to the view that we live in a patriarchy. I'm not sure it's a commonly held belief. I bring it up socially quite regularly (much to my husband's chagrin) and it does provoke fairly scornful reactions.

I know I didn't always think this way. As a Ford graduate trainee and one of the few women they'd ever hired, as a graduate trainee I remember being interviewed by someone writing a book about 'women working in a man's world'. Possibly a book not unlike this one. I was adamant that I didn't detect any sexism in the way I was treated. It makes me cringe (and laugh) now, but out there somewhere is a graduate training brochure featuring me doing the splits across the centrefold. They had wanted to feature the grads doing their hobbies and mine happened to be dancing. All the other guys in the brochure were runners or playing sports and got a page each whereas I had this double page spread of me, legs akimbo in box splits in my leotard. I honestly don't remember thinking there was anything wrong with this. I was certainly unaware of the system. I was one of the young fish that couldn't see the goldfish bowl or the water I was swimming in. Now that was a long time ago, and so I wondered if any woman graduate today would be as guileless as I was then.

The Wolf of Wall Street

I interviewed Zoe, now 30, who had started her career post-university in an all-male financial services outfit that sold tax avoidance schemes. She described it as being like *The Wolf of Wall Street*, only in the UK. Out of the company of 200 people, Zoe can only remember four women and two of them were secretaries. She acknowledges that although it was a 'real lads' culture' she adopted that kind of lads' behaviour. In her own words,

> *You know I was young, it was great fun. I enjoyed the banter element of it but, you know, I was also naïve, and now I look back at some of the things that were said to me and the way I was treated and I would never stand for it today.*

The point I want to make is that when you're in an environment you don't always have the wherewithal to notice or question the culture or the system you are in. You may well even be benefitting from it as I think Zoe and I both did to some extent. We fitted in but we also stood out, which can be helpful early in your career. We didn't question it because we assumed it was the norm.

Going back to my client from the US law firm, I could tell that name-dropping the 'patriarchy' wasn't going to garner much support in the conversation we were having. We were talking about running a women's leadership programme. Rather than seeing the many barriers to women's progress, my client was feeling frustrated because he felt that his firm was already 'bending over backwards' to support women. His expression 'bending over backwards' is telling, as it conjures up a picture of someone having to go out of their 'natural' way to accommodate others. Based on conversations within the firm and their own employee survey, it was clear that this wasn't a view shared by many of the women in the firm, who felt they had a long way to go to meet their needs.

This is a very real problem when it comes to changing the system with respect to gender diversity. Men and women are not coming to the issue with the same perception of the problem or even, in some cases, agreement that there is a problem. My client's expression of frustration is an illustration of how those in the system are predisposed to the status quo. In systems terminology this would be an example of homeostasis, which is defined as 'the self-regulating process by which biological systems tend to maintain stability while adjusting to conditions that are optimal for survival' (Britannica, 2018).

Protecting the system

The desire to maintain the status quo is most keenly felt by the dominant group and so in our society that dominant group is still men, and usually white men, although on this occasion he was a man of colour. On reflection, I think the fact he was a man of colour may have lulled me into assuming he might understand the notion of systems and 'in-groups' and 'out-groups'. This is a mistake I've made on a previous occasion.

I was seated next to a very eminent Anglo-Indian QC at a friend's party when we got to talking about barriers to entry into the judicial system. I had been invited to speak at the Inner Chambers to address a large audience of women barristers some weeks previously, and so felt I would be preaching to the converted when I cited some of the barriers facing women, as I assumed he had faced similar barriers in his own career due to him being a man of colour. I was genuinely taken aback when my dinner companion took pains to reassure me that the training to become a judge was so exemplary that it precluded the possibility of there being any prejudice in the judiciary. He cited his own success as a man of colour as living proof of there being open access for all. This wasn't the picture painted to me at the women barristers conference I had attended just a few weeks previously. It underlined for me that those who rise to the top of a system have a very strong investment in supporting that system and will resist criticism of it; another feature of homeostasis.

Exacerbating the problem is the existence of 'ingroup derogation' where the more oppressed members of outgroups actually put themselves down in comparison with the dominant ingroup. There's a very famous black doll, white doll experiment which is a very poignant example of this in action (Clark and Clark, 1950). I would encourage you watch the video. The experiment involved showing a young Black child two dolls, one black and one white, and then off camera he is asked which of the dolls is the good doll. The expression on the child's face is hard to describe and painful to watch as he resignedly points to the white doll and says that is the good doll. Even at a young age, he was already displaying ingroup derogation where those in the 'outgroup' derogate their own 'in-group'.

Women can also show signs of in-group derogation when they push for coaching that makes women more assertive, more dominant, more like men. In other words, adhering to the leadership norms of the 'in-group'.

We all uphold the system

It's a mistake to think that it's only white men that uphold the patriarchal system. We are all socialised into the system, and men and women alike have grown up under the same set of patriarchal values that has institutionalised gender roles baked in. Although overt gender discrimination is rarely in evidence, what remains is so-called 'second-generation gender bias', which is more subtle and often manifests in organisational design and policy.

Take, for example, when we first launched Parental Transition Coaching in 2005. We called it Maternity Coaching. This is a perfect example of unwittingly reinforcing existing gender norms by seemingly suggesting that only women become parents. We changed it soon afterwards to Parental Transition Coaching to make the point that it's not just women who become parents and to reinforce the importance of recognising fathers. But it's a good example of how unconscious bias affects us all, even those of us keenly aware of its existence and trying to address it.

The broken bridge

As a result of the subtle but pervasive nature of 'second-generation gender bias' it is hard to pin down the problem and therefore hard to gain agreement and build support for solutions among women. To illustrate this problem, I use the concept of describing women's career track as being like a broken bridge. It looks fine at the start, it is ruptured in the middle and then, for those that make it over, it looks fine to most of them too. Let me explain.

Stepping onto the bridge

Many people I talk to about how change will happen assume that young people will make it happen. However, young people are just as susceptible to the power and rewards of the system as anyone else. Like the young fish, young women are also blind to systemic bias just as I was when I worked for Ford. I fitted into an environment where men prevailed and felt I benefitted from being a woman. I was full of optimism about the progress of women, being as I was one of the few women graduate trainees at the Ford Company. I had stepped onto a bridge that for me stretched out invitingly ahead and I could never have imagined that one day I would be writing about how that bridge is broken.

However, my generation's hope for gender parity has not materialised. Nonetheless, the optimism of youth prevails and women's concerns at this stage are very much the same as their male colleagues. How do I make my way across this bridge, to which I've not just been allowed full access, but been warmly welcomed? The lack of role models, sub-optimal task assignment, benevolent bias, male-oriented networking activities and an agentic management style, all forms of second-generation bias, go largely unnoticed or at least unquestioned at this stage. The scenery changes dramatically when they reach the middle of the bridge.

The rupture in the bridge

Because I left a corporate career before becoming a mother, I didn't experience the rupture in the bridge personally when I had my son Cameron. I had already set up ECC and so I was able to flex my work around him and the issue of being 'mummy-tracked' couldn't arise. It is only through coaching women at this critical juncture that I began to appreciate the scale of the challenges they face. Reconciling being the ideal employee and the ideal mother is discombobulating and used to result in a great exodus of women. The bridge truly was broken at that stage with many professional women leaving corporate careers.

However, companies have introduced many strategies for smoothing women's passage and nowadays few actually leave at this stage. There are a number of excellent books which outline many of the systemic interventions that HR departments can consult to ensure they are covering the ground – including Iris Bohnet's 2018 *What Works* and Maitland and Steele's 2020 *INdivisible*.

The introduction of Parental Transition Coaching has made a big difference, as have attitudes to flexible working, and nowadays far fewer women leave their jobs when they become mothers. However, many go part-time and since going part-time is still seen as being less career-committed, many find themselves in the slow lane (or the 'mummy-track') and too few accelerate again to join those women on the other side of the bridge, which is the track to leadership.

I'm at risk of over-extending the metaphor here, but bear with me. The problem with those arriving at the ruptured stage in the bridge is that they are so busy navigating the barriers that they don't have time to even notice the bridge, let alone be vocal about the need for repair. In my experience, few women at this stage in their careers have the time or inclination to advocate on behalf of women, so intent are they on just hanging in there. Life's juggle as a parent uses up a lot of bandwidth and women tend to drop all but the essentials in their job just to keep the show on the road. They also tend to internalise the problems as being signs that they can no longer keep up and so some pull over into the slow lane and others run themselves ragged trying to do everything. Some still leave but they don't stop working, they instead start their own businesses or join companies with more conducive climates in which to progress. I have noticed that these have been often the more entrepreneurial of the women I've coached, ones with a good network that their companies might have benefitted from. Very few make it across to the other side of the bridge still accelerating at the same pace.

The winners

On the other side of the bridge are those women that have 'made it', i.e. they're on the leadership track or have now become leaders. I find they fall broadly into two camps:

1 **Supporters** – Those that succeeded and are still broadly supportive of the bridge because they think, 'I made it therefore so can others'. I've been in a number of meetings where male leaders happily concede the floor to a few women in the room who have battled their way across and seem unwilling to concede any ground when it comes to change. The men in the room defer to them to be the overt defenders of the status quo, while they can follow in the slipstream. There are others who might see the problems with the bridge but don't see the benefit of allying themselves to the 'women's cause'. Like Ellie in Chapter 4, they have got sick of talking to women about women's things. They want to be seen as a 'businessperson' rather than a 'woman in business'. After all, it's risky when you're at the top to ally yourself with the outsider group.

2 **Advocates for change** – The other group, who have also made it to the other side and still on the leadership track, get that it's not working and want to see the bridge being rebuilt and feel frustrated at the slow pace of change. In my experience, these women really are exceptional. How they have managed to cross the bridge and still have the energy and selflessness to be advocates for redesigning it to ensure more women cross it, is deserving only of our admiration in my opinion. So therefore, I can only imagine that it must be galling when they do this work and younger women then describe them as 'exceptional' but not in a positive way, i.e. they are 'exceptional' in that they are not typical, and worse still, 'anti-role models'.

At times I have found it demoralising when I've been talked down by younger women who don't see the problem, thinking that it's yesterday's issue, or by older contemporaries who think women should just 'man up' and get on with it. It frustrates me that this leaves stranded those in the middle stage of their career who simply haven't got the bandwidth to lend their voices to the debate. I'm sure change would happen so much more quickly if all women aligned on the problem. If we are not aligned on the problem, then how can we expect to engage men in resolving it? I talk more about engaging men as stakeholders in Chapter 8.

And so, what can we as coaches do about the broken bridge?

Implications for coaching

To be able to coach women effectively, it is important to highlight the influence that the system plays on their career progression at each stage. Women need to understand that the bridge is faulty and it's not them that's faulty. Failure to alert them to this will result in women re-doubling their efforts to access the leadership track, internalising the blame when they don't succeed and gradually and then abruptly going off the whole idea of leadership.

In Figure 7.1 I've overlaid the Mainiero and Sullivan research (2006) with our expanded ECC 'Six Stages of a Woman's Career' model to show how the focus changes for women as they move through their careers. I will now show how coaching can bring into consciousness the existence of the system in different ways at these three phases.

Bringing the system into focus at the early phase

If women are not made aware of patriarchal systemic bias, then there is a danger that coaching will encourage and reinforce the agentic qualities more commonly associated with men. This early phase is critical to leader identity construction, and if they look up and see mainly male leaders they will assume that to get on that's how you have to behave. For some, with a more agentic style, this will prove attractive, not yet foreseeing the drawbacks experienced by their more agentic senior women colleagues who begin to pick up negative

Figure 7.1 Competing complexities in female career stages

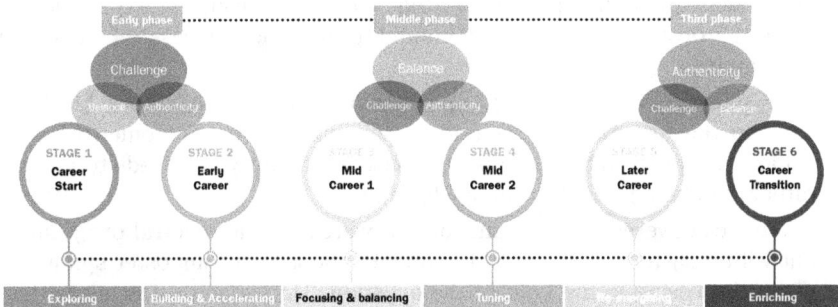

feedback for not displaying sufficient prosocial behaviours as outlined in Chapter 3 in the example of Milly. For others, with a more communal style, they will be put off. For all of them, the paucity of women as role models at the top will be problematic because, as I pointed out in Chapter 4, it's hard to be what you can't see.

In the absence of suitable role models, they will look to the women slightly ahead of them and notice the flatlining of the careers of those who have arrived at the ruptured middle of the bridge. One woman associate lawyer described it as watching her heroes going to the front-line and returning to work seriously wounded. As the Mainiero and Sullivan research shows, the search for balance has tended to come earlier to women and so many will be starting to wonder how they make it all work if they decide to have a family. And so, they will start to 'leave before they leave' as Sheryl Sandberg (2014) famously described it. Coaching at this stage is critical.

What you need to be cognisant of when designing coaching interventions in the early phase

- For a start I believe young women need a women-only space and so group coaching is advisable. I think it gives them the opportunity to experiment with stepping into their own leadership identity and share experiences to learn from each other. Of course they must also feel the psychological safety necessary to discuss the possibility of leaving too. Many women feel the pull of doing something more entrepreneurial and might consider the occasion of becoming a mother as a useful juncture to consider this.
- It is imperative that you ensure any training you are involved with that is women-only training is not conceived as a 'fix the women' solution. A way of doing this is to have the involvement of line managers and sponsors, but rather than as purveyors of wisdom, they need to be signed up in a reverse-mentoring dynamic. Here the managers and sponsors get involved to learn as much as to teach. Ideally the sponsors and managers would have KPIs (key performance indicators) attached to their success in sponsoring talented women coming through. I would go further and propose coaching of the managers and sponsors so that they learn from the experience of being involved and take accountability for the success of diversity programmes.
- The women participating in group coaching should be encouraged to feed-back to the organisation their ideas for ensuring more women become leaders. In this way they are being consulted about what needs to change rather than being asked to change to fit in.
- The topics covered are the same as if it were a gender-neutral programme but with a systemic lens. So, for example, the issue of imposter syndrome needs discussing in the light of the question, 'Do women suffer more than men or do they just discuss it more openly?'

Bringing the system into focus at the middle phase

The problems with the system may become apparent to some women as soon as they are pregnant. This is usually but not exclusively the trigger for going into the search for balance. It's when they describe in coaching sessions how they've started to feel smaller even though they have grown bigger, as they get overlooked for key meetings or for assignments they would have expected to have been given. For some they feel the 'rumble of the system' when they find that parenting is not quite as joint an endeavour as they had anticipated, when their partner struggles to make anti-natal visits because of work pressure.

Here it's important to challenge what she might see as accepted norms and encourage her to have honest conversations with her manager about assumptions they might be making, e.g. that she needs to 'just focus on her family for now'. Some women prefer to get on with the job and not focus too much on being pregnant while others appreciate that kind of consideration. Keeping communication channels open with their manager is key and so is asserting what works for them. This is also the stage to introduce the concept of conscious co-parenting. Couples are usually unconsciously writing the script of how their joint responsibilities will pan out, even before the baby has arrived.

Once the baby arrives, and after the appreciation of the scale of the change has sunk in, the coaching needs to help her welcome her new mother identity and add it to her career identity. Having her focus on the longer term and the role of work in her future is helpful at this stage. Once back at work, helping her to recognise that the skills she learned while on maternity leave were a crash course in leadership can help with the necessary career-revalidation crucial at this early stage. As the VAST model showed in Chapter 4, it is the company that is on trial when she's back, as she calibrates and re-calibrates the sacrifices and returns to assess whether it's all worth it. Coaching can help her and her manager make this transition smoother.

What you need to be cognisant of when designing coaching interventions at the middle phase

- That Parental Transition Coaching works. It makes 'saves' for corporates on a daily basis.
- The importance of coaching the managers; insist on this because otherwise you are fixing the women.
- How to challenge when you see examples of unconscious bias and understanding its subtle but pervasive impact.
- When offering Parental Transition Coaching it has to be offered to fathers too. They are also parents.

- When coaching men, encourage them to take parental leave and to honour men's leave.
- How to introduce the concept of the 'broken bridge' to leaders and stimulate their interest in fixing it.

Bringing the system into focus in the third phase

After the 'tuning' phase of mid-career, where women start to tune into their career wavelength again, comes the third phase where women can feel re-energised and, if fulfilled, go on to an enriching phase where the emphasis is on giving back. This corresponds to Erik Erikson's seventh stage of his Eight Stages of Man model (1993), which he describes as 'regenerative' and Mainiero and Sullivan describe as the search for authenticity (2006).

As described earlier in Chapter 2, this is when women seek work that chimes with their values and where they feel they can express themselves more fully. This might involve re-framing their role and contribution to reflect a newfound desire to shape it to their requirements rather than have it shaped for them.

It also coincides with the menopause, when the body ceases to be fertile with hot flushes and mind blanks playing havoc with women's confidence. Recent research has shown an exodus of women from corporate jobs with many citing menopause symptoms as the cause. Better medical support and less stigma about talking about the menopause can go a long way to stall that exodus. However, this phase also involves a significant identity transition where coaching can play an important role.

What you need to be cognisant of when designing coaching interventions for women at the third phase

- That group coaching for senior women works because it encourages them to develop another network and alliance outside the board room where they may still be in the minority. A coaching network differs from an informal network because it is explicitly focusing on the issue of gender, allowing women to discuss ways for countering any second-generation bias they might be experiencing and take solace from realising they're not alone. It's also an excellent way to exchange tips and advice from other women facing similar challenges.
- The importance of encouraging senior women to sponsor women beneath them rather than simply mentoring them. Women have been found to make better mentors than sponsors, whereas it's the opposite for men. Men take more risks on advocating for others, whereas women focus more on ensuring fairness and so tend to be more likely to mentor than sponsor junior women coming through (Macbride, 2021).

- How reverse mentoring by younger women can provide useful insights from which senior women can learn.
- How to address the 'anti-role model' phenomenon.
- That women at this stage may be interested in getting involved in the company's CSR/ESG (corporate social responsibility/environmental, social, governance) activities as these can help in providing a purpose beyond the day job and play to their desire to 'give back'.

I have explained in this chapter what the system is and what makes it hard to change, and I have provided key stages where coaching interventions can make women more aware of the system and looked at how, by joining forces, they can repair the broken bridge on which they find themselves. I have also highlighted what coaches need to bear in mind from a systemic perspective when coaching women at the different stages of their career. One might say that HR are the custodians of the bridge and in this respect it's incumbent upon them to push for change. Many have worked tirelessly to introduce HR policies that smooth the transition to leadership for women or, for that matter, anyone with caring responsibilities. Recently, many UK organisations have announced equal parental leave, for example, which will go a long way to getting rid of the 'mummy-track' for good. However, some of my HR colleagues (who, in the main are women) have described feeling apprehensive about advocating for women for fear of it being seen as coming from self-interest. And of course, policy can only go so far. Cultural change is necessary for people to feel they can take advantage of family-friendly policies. For this reason, I see men as still being the true custodians of the bridge, as they are still in a majority in leadership. They set the tone and the culture. In the next chapter, I will look at how we can engage men in our quest to build something more fit for purpose.

8 Engaging men

In this chapter I want to talk about how we engage men in a quest for a more gender equal world. I consider whether, by encouraging men to tap into their emotional needs, we can help create a shared vision of the future where 'taking charge' is not seen as the 'go to' style for leaders. By coaching the managers of those going through the parental transition, we can highlight instances of unconscious bias and help them smooth women's return to work. I introduce the notion that some managers 'just get it' when it comes to knowing how to treat new parents who are juggling their lives and outline what that looks like. And finally, I summarise the coaching implications with respect to engaging men in pushing for more gender equity.

Firstly, indulge me as I take a trip down memory lane. I have an incredibly strong memory of a story I read in my school reader (the Janet and John series – that beacon of gender neutrality!) which was all about a competition between the sun, the rain and the wind. They were competing to see who could remove a man's coat as he was walking. I think I was about six years old, and it must have been the first time that I realised that a story could have meaning as well as a narrative because I remember being profoundly affected by it. The fact that the sun won the competition by simply coming out from behind a cloud despite all the violence and dominance of the wind and the rain, who both failed to get the man to take off his coat, made quite an impression on me. The man in the story just held his coat ever tighter as the wind and the rain did their worst. The sun, painted in the illustration with a big beatific smile on its face seemed to do very little at all and yet the man obligingly took his coat off. I think it is quite a fitting parable for how we might engage more men in the quest for gender equality. We need to think sun and not wind and rain.

Gender wars

I considered the title 'Men as allies' for this chapter, but then rejected it because it promotes the idea that there's a war to be won. Taking an oppositional stance and reducing any dialogue to a zero-sum game is rarely effective in my experience and has connotations of a rain and wind approach. Indeed, when I find myself slipping into didactic mode, I can hear the little mantra in my head that says, 'If you insist, they resist'. People don't like to be pushed into change. The sun approach for me is about having people volunteer to join in rather than being forced to. Or another less lyrical way of saying this is that you have to consider the WIIFM (what's in it for me) factor. In this case, 'What's in it for men?'

I believe there's much to be gained by both men and women in a world that doesn't conflate emotionality with so-called feminine traits and strength and power with so-called masculine traits.

And so, to engage men in the topic of gender diversity, the sun approach means avoiding culpability. Instead, we need to be empathic to the needs of men and highlight the considerable benefits of a world that frees them from the obligation to always be the strong person in the room.

In my capacity as Events Co-Chair of City Women's Network (CWN) we have run lots of events around the subject of gender diversity and rarely attract many men. So, we decided to name one of our events 'What about the Men?' and assembled an all-male panel. We had our largest turnout of men at that event that I've been privy to during my eight years at CWN. It was a fascinating discussion and showed how one shouldn't imagine for a minute that all men think the same about the topic of gender diversity. Just like women, there was a huge divergence of opinion about the best way to go about change, but it was notable that they were all in favour of change.

Barriers to men's participation in the diversity agenda

I think most men want to get it right when it comes to gender equality. A survey by Fairygodboss (2019) interviewed 400 men and found that 88 per cent want to help women advance in the workforce but don't know the best actions to take. Even if they wanted to be advocates, they lack the knowledge to do so. A Catalyst study (Prime and Moss-Racusin, 2009) highlighted the barriers to men acting as advocates for gender equality under three categories:

1 **Fear**. A lot of men are very wary of saying the wrong thing when around women and they worry about ridicule from fellow men if they are seen to be upstanders too.
2 **Ignorance**. Either real or perceived. They feel they don't know the subject well enough and tread carefully around women, deferring to them as being more expert.
3 **Apathy**. They're just not sure what's in it for them.

I think this is where the sun needs to come in. We need to paint an inspiring and inviting vision of what the future could look like so that men and women alike are inspired – one which recognises that men and women are not so different in what they need to be happy. The patriarchy might have been designed by men for men, but it's worth noting that it may no longer be working for all men.

What about the men?

I feel strongly that men are caught between the archetypes of old and the pressures of today. We can see their unhappiness manifest in a number of worrying statistics. Suicide is the biggest killer of men under the age of 50. This compares to a much lower rate for women (Sutherland, 2018). There are far more men in prison, more men are addicts, more boys are medicated, and the rising knife crime rate in the UK is testament to a system that seems to be failing many men. Of course, I recognise that I've pulled my focus back and I'm now panning out to look at society as a whole and not specifically on those men in the corporate world in which I coach. It's true that the male leaders I coach are more likely to be beneficiaries of the current system and, as they set the standards for those below them in the organisation, what they think has a disproportionate impact and yet it may not always reflect the views of the wider community of men.

Cracks are beginning to show here too. Men in corporate life are also challenging what makes a successful life. Many conclude that they have sacrificed too much of their personal lives in their pursuit of a career. Those men at the top who are now facing retirement do not all welcome the prospect of a cliff-edge end to their gainful employment and are now seeking part-time solutions where they can pursue portfolio careers. This brings them closer to the thinking of their very much younger male colleagues who enter the workforce seeing flexibility as a basic human right.

The ONS track wellbeing and although men report less stress than women, they do come up short on overall happiness with life when compared to women (Tabor and Stockley, 2018). Women have been described as the 'canaries down the coalmine', as in they have smelt the toxic gases first, and this partly explains why so few pursue the route to leadership. They haven't opted out of the leadership track but have been eased out by a system that may have overlooked their potential or not focused sufficiently on their needs – needs that are straightforward and understandable for all humans. They want to live a full life, which involves a fulfilling career and a rich home life. I believe this is also what men want and I see coaching as a way to help them achieve that.

What do men want?

I think we are going through something of a masculinity crisis. Having been brought up to be strong and obey the 'men don't cry' mantra, we have unwittingly made it off limits for men to emote. As I write this, England managed to get to the finals of the European football tournament but failed to win against Italy in the end. Throughout the tournament I've been struck by how much male fans do emote. But they seem constrained to a very narrow band of emotions, mainly featuring elation or anger. It's as if they are not taught to comfort each other easily. Most of them stood in silent disbelief when the other side won. The cameras panned over thousands of men standing silently looking on grimly but not turning to each other. And unfortunately, anger overwhelmed many too, who resorted to violence after the match.

It was a stark and surprising contrast to all this untrammelled or suppressed emotion to witness the example of the team manager who immediately went to comfort the three desolate England players who had missed penalties. Much was made of the England manager's unusually inclusive approach to building what has been the most successful squad for some time in England. He role modelled empathy and humility throughout the tournament; both leadership qualities which are essential for this better, shared vision of the world that I think will make both men and women happier. This is a world which needs a more empathic and compassionate approach, and this need is ever more acute in the face of advancing technological innovation.

Man against the machine

Technology is getting ever more sophisticated and capable of replicating human endeavour to a degree I don't think any of us could have foreseen. Even the professions are seeing some of their professional territory being nibbled away by computers. A lot of the procedural stuff like wills, bookkeeping and even diagnosing our own illnesses can be done online.

As computers take over repetitive and mundane tasks, making swathes of clerical people redundant in their wake, there is a concomitant growth for jobs in the caring sector. Nurses, teachers, physiotherapists, psychologists, coaches are all going to be in demand. What's interesting is how the core skill of caring is a prerequisite for all these jobs. There's a case to be made for caring being the one key skill that computers can't replicate.

It's ironic therefore that most caring jobs are done by women and tend to be underpaid. Much of the domestic load plus childcare and eldercare that currently falls to women is completely unpaid. I think we will see this changing in time as an ageing population places greater emphasis on these skills. It will be interesting to watch the remuneration go up as more men enter the caring professions.

For now, the caring professions are currently staffed in the main by women and people of colour, i.e. a diverse workforce, and so it will be incumbent upon leaders to understand how to engage this diversity as these caring skills jump from the third sector and into the business world.

To care is to be human

This will necessitate a shift in leadership style to one that's more inclusive and underpinned by empathy, compassion and collaboration – if you like, a move to be more human. These are the communal traits more commonly associated with and encouraged for women and seen as 'soft skills' or 'feminine traits'.

The prevailing leadership style of dominance, assertion and knowledge seem no longer as effective in our world of diverse networks, flat hierarchies, empowered staff and shared knowledge. A new set of skills is required for leading inclusively. Key to any organisation's success is the engagement of its people and engaging people isn't the same as telling them what to do. It will therefore require some unlearning on the part of existing leaders. I think this is where coaching can make a significant difference, because we can role model and encourage men and those women who share the same leadership style to explore a new style of engaging, one which shifts from knowing to asking, from expert to enquiry, from strong to vulnerable – if you like, to use a more sun approach.

Old-school macho man leadership

In all my years of coaching I've actually coached very few old-school command-and-control style leaders. I doubt many of them sign up for coaching. However, I have coached a few men (and a few women) that have been 'made' to have coaching because their style was deemed to be erring on the aggressive side.

I'm going to introduce you to Daniel now because he displayed all the stereotypical 'masculine' traits in abundance, and so is a good example to highlight how being socialised as a strong, dominant man can start to work against you in today's world and how coaching can help to unpick that style and show a different way to lead. The coaching was offered to him, but he felt he had no choice but to go along with it and so the coaching didn't start off in the best way. It's often inadvisable to take on coachees who feel they 'have' to be coached. It sets up a parent/child dynamic when what you need is an adult/adult one. I was keen to have an initial chemistry session first.

Box 8.1 DANIEL'S STORY

Daniel ran a number of depots for a major delivery firm. He was in his fifties and had worked his way up from the shop floor. The working environment was what Daniel might describe as a stereotypically 'man's world'. Very few women to speak of, and those that were there, were in HR or support functions. To meet him for the first time in person was to see part of the 'diagnosed problem' writ large. He was an enormously imposing man with a loud, booming voice and a handshake like a vice. His bark was much worse than his bite and I warmed to him in our chemistry check.

He was open and funny and very direct; a fellow Northerner, so I felt at ease with this bluntness. He was mortally wounded by the accusation that his style could be perceived as overbearing, even bullying, and had seen himself in a very different light. Friends and family would describe him as having a heart of gold and being a big softie underneath the bluff exterior. He was mortified and indignant that he'd been assigned a coach, but by hearing him out non-judgementally I believe he felt he could trust me enough to engage in coaching. On meeting him I felt that he could use some 'sun'.

Role modelling a coaching style

We covered a lot of ground in the coaching sessions, and I know Daniel appreciated my challenge laced with support. I could empathise with the fact that his larger-than-life persona had served him well up until this point and now this had changed, and he was starting to pick up negative feedback about being domineering. Having been praised in the past for his leadership traits, he now found it hard to see a need for change. It was important to empathise with his frustration that what got him to the level he was at was no longer working for him.

I took pains to acknowledge with him that the world around us has changed and that's why we all need to adapt to stay relevant. Being curious and listening intently to his view of the world and how his situation had unfolded, and truly empathising with it, gave me licence to move into more challenging territory. In doing so I was consciously modelling a coaching style. He was able to notice that I could be challenging and yet I was mainly asking questions. He realised that he was having to work harder when I left silence and didn't jump to fill it in. Had I been in any way judgemental, or had I tried to advocate for a different style of leadership, he would have immediately been on guard, with his defences up. However, using a probing and understanding style, Daniel could experience how he was given space to think and that he was able to reach new conclusions about his leadership style without input from me. He was getting there on his own. He just needed some in-the-moment feedback.

Size does matter

I don't think Daniel had any idea of the impact his stature had over the dynamics in his exchanges with others. He had such a loud voice that one of my team popped in at one point to offer coffee to check I was OK, thinking he was shouting at me. Sharing that with him, with a degree of humour, was the perfect feedback opportunity to help illustrate that his size and loud voice alone could be experienced as overpowering, even frightening. This was at odds with his intention, which was to solve problems for everyone. We discussed how his need to solve problems for everyone, which was a manifestation of his kindness, could unintentionally disempower those that work with him. I introduced the notion of power 'with' as opposed to power 'over', which made him think about his power in the context of his family.

Parallels with family life

We found that a useful perspective to help him examine his leadership style came from his relationship with his teenage children. Daniel saw himself as a protector and the children were pushing back against this, seeing it as coming from a need to control rather than to nurture. This really helped as a parallel for his paternalistic/hero leadership style. He soon got the point that he was impeding their learning by restricting his children so much. What helped him see this was when he reflected on those times where he had learned most himself. He realised that it was often when he was trusted to learn from his mistakes. Being trusted was a crucial part of the learning. It made him rise to the occasion and do things he wasn't sure he could do.

When Daniel applied this realisation to how he leads his people at work, he could see that he was protecting his team from failure but was robbing them of the opportunity to learn. His own risk aversion to failure was being channelled into his team who, in turn, were not taking risks for fear of getting it wrong. His 'take charge' instinct coupled with his imposing stature wasn't creating a psychologically safe place in which his people could flourish. When people's threat instinct is triggered, their cognitive function narrows to deal with the threat. Rather than inspiring those around him, Daniel was inhibiting them from coming up with their best ideas.

Drawing out Daniel's capacity for 'taking care' not 'taking charge'

In a way, when I was coaching Daniel, I was aware that I was coaching him to be less stereotypically masculine, to be less of a hero leader. So much of his style emanated from the scripts he'd absorbed as a child about having to be strong, take control, be right. I was coaching him to reframe being 'responsible for' others to being 'respons-able' to others. To use more pull and less push. I was helping him to unlearn some of the skills that had got him into his leadership position in the first place. To be vulnerable, in Daniel's mind, was to be weak and so we focused on leaders that he considered strong who were comparatively mild-mannered. We considered examples of where someone being vulnerable was experienced as a demonstration of strength. By toning down his 'masculine' traits I was able to tune into his strong empathic side, his 'heart of gold'. We worked on how he could re-frame caring, not through being the saviour and taking charge, but by helping others to help themselves.

Focusing on purpose

When I think back on my coaching of Daniel, I realise that I didn't introduce notions of gender differences at all into our coaching sessions. I believe that would have made him see our conversations in a different light, perhaps my light. I think by sticking to a conversation about what would give him great pleasure in life, i.e. his purpose, which was having a more fruitful relationship with his teenage children, we were also able to tackle the aspects of his leadership style that were undermining his effectiveness and making him unhappy.

Tackling the system

I think by doing this work I am helping to promote the gender agenda because I'm tackling the system by helping leaders such as Daniel to move from a paternalistic style of leadership to an inclusive style. I'm challenging their received world view by introducing an alternative frame of reference. But I'm not imposing it. I'm tapping into what matters for them and having them consider if their approach is working for them.

Again, I must stress that it's not just men that have learned a paternalistic style of leadership. Women leaders too are shaped by society's habit of conflating leadership with the agentic behaviours usually associated with men. Highlighting the importance of the mantra 'Seek first to understand before being understood' is relevant for all leaders.

I will return to this topic in the next chapter, where I will flesh out further what I mean by inclusive leadership, but first I would like to cover another way to engage men in changing the system.

I believe that including managers in Parental Transition Coaching has benefits beyond those that parents receive. I see it as a window of opportunity to reach out to managers, and allay their fears, address blind spots in their knowledge and, in some cases, tackle the apathy they may feel towards changing the status quo. I see it as an opportunity to help them reconsider the way work is constructed and help make the changes conducive to richer personal lives for all. It's also an opportune time to pick up unconscious bias in action.

Making the link between changing the system and Parental Transition Coaching

Research carried out by Kathy Cotter (2016) on the impact of maternity coaching highlighted how significant the manager's involvement is. Ninety-three per cent of those interviewed agreed with the statement 'to maximize the effectiveness of maternity coaching, line-managers should also be coached in managing women returners'.

Managers' attitudes can have a profound effect on the success of a parent's successful transition back to work following the birth of a child. Coaching managers is such an important part of the 'fix the system, not the women' approach that we advise clients to make it compulsory.

As in all coaching, asking open-ended questions is the go-to method for establishing the perspective and experience of the person being coached. Opening with whether they have experience of managing someone going through this transition is a good place to start. This often leads into them describing their own experience of parenting or their impressions of what's involved. This is where unconscious bias can be detected at an individual level. This is often in the form of 'benevolence bias'. Here is a definition:

> Benevolence bias occurs when our efforts to be kind result in us making decisions on other people's behalf that take away their choices. Put another way, benevolence bias is when we limit an individual's autonomy by presuming what's best for them. (Bond, 2018)

And here is an example.

Benevolence bias in action

I recently coached a manager who works in banking and was managing a very ambitious young Black woman who was about to return from maternity leave. He was a very keen advocate of diversity and was very keen to impress upon me the lengths he'd gone to ensure his direct report was put forward for promotion following her maternity leave. In the conversation, he mentioned that he felt able to put her forward because she was a 'bullet proof candidate'. When I enquired further, he explained that 'obviously, with a Black female candidate she had to be twice as good as anyone else so no one would accuse him of just trying to tick the diversity box'. I played back his words to him and asked did that mean that he wouldn't promote minority candidates if they were simply equal to white, male candidates?

The penny dropped for this manager that he was setting the bar higher because he was fearful of the scrutiny that minority candidates attract and wanted to protect his direct report, but in doing so he was unwittingly harming other marginalised parties looking for promotion. I explained that this was a form of benevolence bias, a term he hadn't come across, and he was appalled that he'd been victim to this unconscious bias despite having attended mandatory unconscious bias training and thinking of himself as 'one of the good guys'.

Business risk

One-to-one coaching with managers allows for every conversation to be tailored to the unique experience and perspective of each manager. As a coach you can tune into that person's wavelength and meet them where they are. In this respect I see it as an effective tool for drawing out and allaying managers' fear of getting this stuff wrong, and coaches can build on the unconscious bias training that most managers have now attended by making it personal. I also think it's a business risk to allow managers to get it wrong.

Some managers just 'get it'

Of course, there are managers who don't get it wrong and seem to just 'get it'. I find primary carers often 'get it' irrespective of gender. It's about having had the experience of significant time off with a baby. However, some managers who have not had that experience just 'get it' too. I've tried to crystallise what 'getting it' means. For me, it boils down to those that know how to ask questions and not make assumptions about what type of support new parents might need. These are the managers that recognise that people vary enormously and don't rely on rule-of-thumb thinking when it comes to how they treat people who are going through the significant life experience of bringing a new baby into the world or welcoming a new baby into their home. So, for example, a manager that just 'gets it' reaches out to men too to check in with how they're doing rather than fall back on banter as their only means of communication with expectant dads. These are the managers that also don't make gendered assumptions about who the primary carer is and are cognisant that not all partnerships are heteronormative. It's an inclusive way of thinking.

We have an excellent video interview with a male law firm partner on the 'Work, Family and You' part of our website (ECC, 2021). In it, Jim, part of a same-sex couple who engaged a surrogate to have their child, gives advice to managers about the best way to be in these circumstances. I encourage you to watch it. An important piece of advice he dispenses to managers is to ask questions that are designed to be 'helpful to the prospective parents and not ones to satisfy your curiosity'. I find this to be a golden nugget piece of advice for all managers with direct reports becoming parents, whatever the circumstances. For me it encapsulates so much of what being an inclusive leader entails.

In conclusion

I hope to have shown how men are shaped by the same narrative as women when it comes to gender stereotypes and they are also victims of a system that favours more agentic behaviours. It's important to formulate an appealing vision of the future that benefits men. Michael Kimmel ends his brilliant 2015 Ted Talk 'Why gender equality is good for everyone – Men included' by quoting a 1915 article in an American magazine that declared that 'Feminism will make it possible for the first time for men to be free'. Daniel's story, 100 years later, shows that there's still a way to go. It highlights the challenges for men brought up to believe that taking charge was what was expected of them to now find the script has changed and taking care is taking precedence. And finally, I show how coaching men who are managers of parents is a great opportunity for highlighting examples of unconscious bias and encouraging those managers who just 'get it' to keep on doing what they are doing.

Coaching implications

Being a coach puts us in the privileged position to:

- Alert people to different ways they might respond to a given situation and give them more options
- Have them examine their own stories and see how those have affected how they view the world to reveal the lens they bring to a given leadership scenario
- Uncover instances of unconscious bias, often benevolence bias, and do so in a way that avoids triggering a defensive reaction
- Understand that men's seeming reluctance to getting involved in the gender diversity agenda is often not down to apathy, but to fear or ignorance
- Extend to men the same 'unconditional positive regard' that Carl Rogers espoused some 70 years ago.

In the next chapter, I will expand on what I understand to be inclusive leadership and what it means for coaching.

9 Coaching for inclusive leadership

Having highlighted in the last chapter an example of hero leadership and how this can unintentionally disempower people, I want to examine its successor, inclusive leadership, in more depth. Having worked in the sphere of women's leadership development for the last 15 years, I have become convinced that having inclusive leaders is central to harnessing the potential of not only women but a more diverse workforce per se. Harnessing potential is not simply a recruitment activity. It is pointless to recruit a diverse team unless everyone can feel free to contribute their ideas. In other words, you need to work at being inclusive when you have a diverse team. You can't rely on your own experience to guide you.

In this chapter I will outline why inclusive leadership is important and use a three-circle model of self, others and systems to describe the interplay between these different components. I will focus on the importance of self-compassion for achieving the necessary psychological safety critical for enabling diverse voices to be heard. And finally, I will turn the systems lens inward to consider diversity in the coaching profession.

But first, I want you to imagine that you are suddenly plunged into darkness. What would you do? I can imagine that the first thing that might happen is you slow your pace and use your hands to feel what's near you. All of your other senses would become sharpened. And if you're with other people, you might communicate with them to share your understanding of what's going on. Think now about what it would be like to have someone blind in the room with you. It would give you a wholly different perspective. For a start, they are presumably unperturbed by the lack of light and they have the advantage of their other senses being way more developed to compensate. You would most likely gratefully cede to the leadership of the blind person in this scenario, as they are most familiar with darkness.

I see this as analogous to what it is to lead in today's VUCA world. Change, turbo-charged by technology, resists human attempts to grasp it, let alone control it. Instead, we find ourselves being buffeted by it, constantly surprised by the unpredictable unfolding of events. One day we might find ourselves suddenly in the darkness, where someone unsighted can lead for a bit and then the next, we're in dazzling light but with arctic temperatures where the Inuit person with (in the popular notion) 100 words for snow is in a better position to guide for a while.

Why do I believe in inclusive leadership?

I hope my metaphor of the darkness and the arctic scenario reveals the importance of seeing leadership as something that should move around and is distributed, depending on the circumstances. It is absurd to imagine that one individual can chart the course relying solely on their sense-making apparatus when the world is volatile. It is far wiser to put aside the notion of being a hero leader, uniquely equipped with superhuman insight, as this isn't going to cut it in a constantly evolving world. What we learned yesterday may have worked for yesterday, but not for today. Learning is the new superpower. We need a variety of perspectives to augment our sense-making apparatus, hence we need a diverse team around us and that diversity needs to encompass much more than gender.

Birds of a feather ...

Of course, it's one thing to have a diverse team, but it's quite another to make sure we hear and benefit from those diverse voices and perspectives. In my example, there was a clear and compelling need for different views. In the ambiguity created by darkness, the blind team member came into their own, as did the Inuit perspective in the arctic conditions. But the need for that diversity of perspective is rarely as obviously critical as in my scenario. It's much more tempting to turn to and be influenced by those who think like us. Teams tend to form around coalitions of people that might have shared history, and so, perhaps inevitably, teams err on the homogenous side. Birds of a feather flock together.

It's very seductive as a leader to surround ourselves with people who think very like us because it's more harmonious. We can usually arrive at solutions more quickly than if we must marshal differing perspectives. If the problem is simple to resolve, then homogeneity in the team is an advantage. However, the issues we face today are anything but simple. Often the solutions must be conjured on the spot and require innovative thinking. It requires different perspectives to arrive at creative solutions, hence the need for diversity and for the leader to know how to make different people feel like they belong in order that their ideas are heard.

Figure 9.1 neatly summarises the commercial need for being more diverse and for more inclusive leaders.

The outcomes of inclusive leadership

Ironically, it is probably easier to measure the outcomes of inclusive leadership in how a team 'feels' at work than it is to explain the skills and processes that help a leader create that oft-elusive environment. So, what is an inclusive

Figure 9.1 How inclusive leaders drive organisation growth

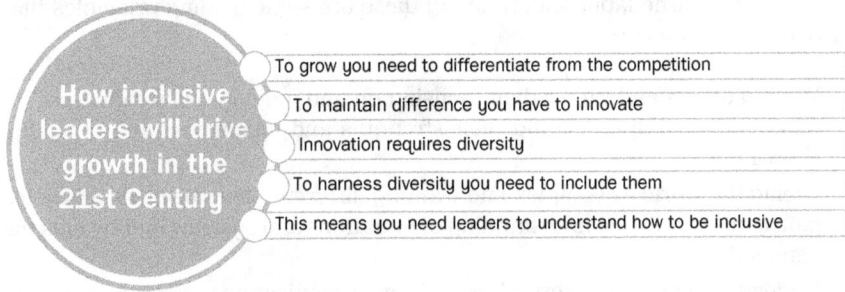

How inclusive leaders will drive growth in the 21st Century	
	To grow you need to differentiate from the competition
	To maintain difference you have to innovate
	Innovation requires diversity
	To harness diversity you need to include them
	This means you need leaders to understand how to be inclusive

environment? It essentially comes down to whether the team members feel like they belong and are 'safe' to be themselves – so-called 'psychological safety'.

I think 'safe to be themselves' barely captures the scale of benefits and implications for the individual, team, and organisation. It is perhaps more accurate to say that the individual feels 'valued' for who they are, for their uniqueness. They are valued as whole, imperfect human beings as we all are. This value extends to capture not only race, gender, sexuality or any other protected characteristic, but crucially to our strengths and our faults, quirks, insecurities, doubts and so on. It is why being cognisant of how our tendency to stereotype denies our very uniqueness and prevents us feeling valued is so crucial.

Google ran a project called Aristotle that examined thousands of meetings to establish what made them successful, and they identified the unifying component was 'psychological safety'. They characterised the behaviours required as 'conversational turn-taking and empathy'. Amy Edmondson (2014) a professor of leadership and management at Harvard business school explains the outcomes of creating psychological safety: '[T]eam members feel they can speak up with concerns, bad news, or ideas without fear of being shut down, blamed, or humiliated'. Imagine the improvement in decision-making that occurs with this enrichment in perspectives, challenge and information.

Of course, as coaches, we know well the power for our clients when we create psychological safety by offering them acceptance, empathy and trust. It was noticeable how Daniel opened up because he felt that I was listening. That's when we see our clients flourish and where they can more easily look to themselves to solve problems, be creative, be honest with themselves, fail, learn, retry, evolve and the list goes on. Therein lies the power of inclusive environments.

And inclusive leadership?

I think of inclusive leadership at its foundation as a philosophy. That is to say, 'a set of beliefs or an attitude to life that guides somebody's behaviour' (Oxford Dictionary, 2022). It does involve skills, like asking questions and active listening, and embraces Carl Rogers' probing and understanding behaviours too. These skills can be learned, but underpinning these are some guiding principles that have to be embraced:

- Valuing others and rather than focusing on and judging the 'weaknesses' of others, instead appreciating their strengths and uniqueness and crucially, showing it.
- Seeing the world as complex and wanting different views because this helps gain a more holistic understanding of situations and systems and reveals the connections.
- Understanding that hierarchies within organisations are an outdated construct that are less relevant in today's fast-moving and uncertain environment. Knowing complex problems can rarely be resolved alone and appreciating that distributing leadership power will result in greater motivation, innovation, energy and results.

These principles are not traditionally ones that have been cultivated in education and honed in the business world. I notice a more individualistic, competitive approach prevailing where spotting the gaps and weaknesses in arguments has been applauded over collaborative, strengths-based endeavour. It is certainly changing with younger people coming into the workplace, but the patterns and frameworks of old are stubborn and new hires' competitive instincts are still harnessed and fuelled by reward systems that promote internal competition rather than teamwork.

It's not as easy as it sounds

With a cursory glance at these principles, you could be forgiven for thinking that it's a simple fix to become an inclusive leader. But, for many leaders it requires significant unlearning. I know, as a leader and coach for 30 years, that I've had to unlearn a lot:

- My analytical bent trained me to correct things, to spot weaknesses. My experience has shown me, however, that focusing on what's going well and building on that usually pays more dividends. When you apply that to people, focusing on strengths definitely pays off because people perform better when they are engaged. And they are more engaged when they're doing something they are good at.
- I can understand leaders' penchant for making quick decisions rather than consulting more but, again, experience has taught me that you get it wrong when you do that – there are too many interdependencies. It's too big a risk to assume you're right.
- I also know how tempting it is to forge ahead thinking you know where you're going. But as the old saying goes, 'If you want to go quickly, go yourself, but if you want to go far, go together'. It's simply not sustainable to go alone.

Although it may require some unlearning, I do think that inclusive leadership is a movement that's gathering momentum. People may be realising that the old style of hero leadership just doesn't work anymore. I see it as a requirement for all leaders and not just those interested in protecting marginalised employee groups. I think this is an important distinction because, as explained in the (Figure 9.1) model above, there is an economic imperative in addition to a moral imperative for leading inclusively. Leaders need to understand inclusivity as a strategic imperative rather than an annexe to HR issues. For this reason, it's central to my executive coaching work.

How to help coachees be inclusive leaders

Because inclusive leadership is a philosophical approach, you need to work at a deeper level than pure skills training. It involves what's known as 'vertical development'. Vertical development is how we think, feel and make sense of the world. It is about helping people to thrive in constantly evolving work environments. It starts with having leaders look inwards, at what drives them, what 'truths' they have swallowed whole from their childhood. Only then can they look at how these play out in their interactions with others. It's about understanding how intentions and impact correlate when it comes to how they are received. And all of this needs to be seen in the broader context of the culture of their company and the wider environment.

Illustrated in Figure 9.2 is the self, others, systems model that, in my view, best captures the three critical processes to bring to the coaching environment. I've also included coaching questions for each stage. At the core of the three circles is the focus on self. I've made it the largest circle because much of the work is done at this level. The next circle is about how we interact with others and the outside circle represents the systems we operate in, the water in which we swim if you like. They are interdependent and as such you can't work on one in isolation of the others, but I do think in coaching, focusing initially on the self is critical.

Figure 9.2 The self, others, systems model

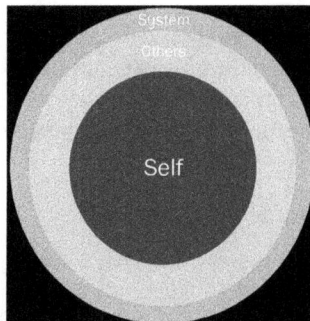

1 Working on the self

When it comes to leading inclusively, perhaps the real question for you and your coachee isn't how to develop inclusive leadership skills but rather, what gets in the way of choosing an inclusive approach? If we think, for example, about our own worst leadership moments, why do we sometimes distrust, judge, compete, defend, disempower, over-simplify, exclude, lack compassion or empathy, and drive for perfection, sacrificing our wellbeing in the process? I think that typically what is happening in these moments is that our threat system has been activated. We are responding too much to our fears, for example, of looking stupid or being judged or of being deemed inadequate or irrelevant. When our amygdala system fires up it is incredibly powerful and, as such, is described as 'amygdala hijack'. It literally takes over the brain.

Our threat system

Once we feel threatened, we can often look to unhealthy ways of defending, avoiding and behaving. As I've highlighted before, this is when our focus narrows and our ability to problem solve declines. I have seen in many coachees how avoidant strategies to feeling threatened can include 'threat-based drive'. This is where you notice a coachee striving for perfection and often becoming hyper-critical of themselves in the process.

I'm increasingly having to start coaching sessions with breathing exercises as people's cortisol levels seem permanently elevated. It's as though they ping-pong between feeling bad about themselves and working ever harder to make themselves feel better, hoping to get a dopamine hit from say, clearing their inbox. But then they find it doesn't make them feel better and they get stuck in a loop of diminishing returns. It's a form of addiction. An excellent article from *The Atlantic* posits that dissatisfaction is our natural state and it's our primordial instincts for survival that urge us to strive for more, work harder and continuously push ourselves harder to make us feel satisfied (Brooks, 2022). However, it's only a short-term fix and so the 'hedonic treadmill' continues.

When I think of the many people I have coached over the years, both men and women, it's apparent that their drive for perfection and tendency to work all hours to hit impossible deadlines is often about feeling the need to prove themselves. It can come from feelings of inadequacy, of not quite measuring up. So many successful people are driven by a fear of failure.

What triggers our individual threat systems can be difficult to untangle. The mind doesn't know the difference between a real and imagined threat so those internal narratives and the stories that we tell ourselves trigger our defences.

Achieving a balanced mind

It's important to help leaders understand how to recognise when this system is activated and how to achieve the 'balanced mind', a term coined by Dr Paul Gilbert:

We have, as human beings, evolved to focus on the threats, the negative and to prepare for the worst to survive and so, we have to work much harder to develop a compassionate and soothing voice for ourselves to achieve this 'balance'. (Gilbert, 2020)

It is this process of self-compassion that allows us to deregulate our threat system so we open our mind and achieve, as Brené Brown would say, a 'grounded confidence' (2018). Cultivating self-compassion allows us to broaden our thinking, not focus on 'the problem' with ourselves; it helps us look at alternatives and be more accepting and forgiving of our limitations.

I like Kristen Neff's definition. She describes self-compassion as: '[C]aring about ourselves – fragile and imperfect yet magnificent as we are. Rather than pitting ourselves against other people in an endless comparison game, we embrace what we share with others and feel more connected and whole in the process' (2011: 153).

Modelling self-compassion

I feel that this goes to the heart of how we, as coaches, can be of service. And so, we must practise this ourselves and part of that is recognising and forgiving ourselves when we fall short and allowing ourselves to be vulnerable. It's also about us acknowledging that we are not the finished article and that we share our common humanity in this respect with our coachees. I'm particularly drawn to the sentence in Neff's quote above where she says, '[W]e embrace what we share with others and feel more connected and whole in the process' (2011: 153). As my example in Chapter 6 demonstrated, when I opened up to my coachee, she felt able to do the same. Being able to talk about something that had gone wrong for me was a sign that I had been able to forgive myself and was no longer too ashamed to vocalise it. In doing this, I was role modelling both vulnerability and self-compassion and normalising failure.

But even as I write this, I find myself wondering, 'Have I been good enough at helping people to soothe themselves in more constructive ways in my coaching? Have I focused enough on self-compassion? Could I have spent more time on these areas?' In other words, I'm not practising the self-compassion I espouse. Old habits die hard. It takes a conscious effort to hush the inner critic, but recognising it and seeing it for just one version of reality, an overly negative one, is a movement in a positive direction. Here, Neff summarises the benefits of self-compassion well:

Self-compassion provides an island of calm, a refuge from the stormy seas of endless positive and negative self-judgment so that we can finally stop asking, 'Am I as good as they are? Am I good enough?' By tapping into our inner wellsprings of kindness, acknowledging the shared nature of our imperfect human condition, we can start to feel more secure, accepted, and alive. (2011: 13)

2 Working on our interaction with others

When something goes wrong, we tend to either berate ourselves or become defensive and blame others. Fear of failure can spill over into our treatment of others. It can manifest overtly in the form of unrelenting demands and harsh judgement or more covertly whereby we bypass or exclude people because we don't 'rate' their contribution. It amounts to the same thing. It robs people of the chance to grow. It is the antithesis of the growth mindset required to keep learning in our ever-changing world. For this reason, it's vital to encourage coachees to practise self-compassion because it is key to softening their judgement of themselves **and** others. Only when we can see failure as a shared human experience will we acquire the balanced approach necessary for being inclusive and allowing others to flourish.

As your coachee begins to develop self-compassion, they will experience improvements in areas like their resilience, problem-solving abilities and energy. It will allow them to access more easily 'open' thinking rather than the 'narrow' thinking driven by unhelpful and fearful beliefs. They will better understand their interaction with others, helping them to be more 'respons-able', as I demonstrated in Daniel's case. From this 'open' and more balanced mind they can connect to others and compassion to self and others becomes easier.

Coming from this balanced place will engender the psychological safety required for leading inclusively. What a psychologically safe space looks like and how to create it can be challenging for leaders to understand off the written page and in the real world.

The coaching relationship is a parallel learning process for your coachee. It's within the coaching conversation that you can role model how to create a safe space for them to open up. In this way they can appreciate the benefits first-hand, as they will appreciate how they have been able to expand their thinking and be more resourceful in finding a solution by being given time to think.

3 The system and systemic thinking

Another leadership behaviour being role modelled in the coaching conversation is the ability to think systemically. This is the vertical development to which I alluded earlier. By raising your coachee's awareness of the systems in which they are operating, you broaden their perspective and give them more options. In the case of Daniel, he experienced the benefit of being listened to compassionately. The absence of judgement and the open-ended questions created enough psychological safety for him to open up. By listening to his story and appreciating the culture that had cultivated the leadership style he was now being asked to change, I was able to reframe the request for him to change his style as being the result of a cultural shift rather than a personal slight, which reduced his defensiveness. This appreciation of the systemic changes happening at a cultural level allowed him sufficient perspective to be able to reconsider his leadership style. It wasn't that he was faulty, it was that the system had changed. By introducing his family, another system in which he was operating, he could make the connection that formed the basis of the 'aha' that helped him see the benefits of change.

To solve problems these days, we can rarely think about simple cause and effect patterns and solutions. Instead, we need to look at the same issue through multiple lenses and build a picture of connections and dependencies. I would go as far as to say that being able to think systemically is a requirement for leaders today. By having Daniel sit back and look at himself systemically I was helping Daniel to question the notion of one 'true' view of any situation or problem. In doing this I was helping him to recognise that there's often a complex system at play in most scenarios. By asking questions I was encouraging and modelling curiosity and collaboration to help him tap into different perspectives and enrich his thinking. I was helping him to see that the system is constantly evolving, and dynamic, and other viewpoints can be as flawed and subjective as his own. I was helping him to reframe feedback as information and not criticism. By encouraging Daniel to take a more holistic view and acknowledge and feel more comfortable with ambiguity, he was better prepared to meet the complexity head-on. In a sense, the coaching conversations eased him away from the habit of quick-fire 'solutioneering' and to embrace more humility in the face of complexity by recognising that issues are multivaried and so it's imperative that you involve others in their resolution.

Turning the lens inwards

Having covered how we need to look at self, others and system when coaching leaders, I'm sure it's self-evident that the same model applies to ourselves as coaches. I know as a coach I'm constantly working on myself and my interaction with others. Of late I've become more interested in questioning the coaching system in which we operate. I've asked myself questions such as: Who is the in-group and who is the out-group when it comes to the coaching community? Who do we ignore and who do we applaud in the coaching world? What's the gender split like? Who charges more? Do we have a gender pay gap situation? How does the coaching profession fare with respect to cultural and ethnic diversity? In other words, I've considered more how the challenges in the wider system are reflected in the coaching system. When I looked at my own company a number of years ago, I realised we were suffering from 'blonde bob syndrome'.

Valuing diversity in the coaching system

I had to face up to the fact to that my leadership team and core team were not diverse. We have made strides with the core team but remain too similar at the top. My coach team looked too similar too. I referred to us disparagingly as the 'blonde bobs' when I sought the help of Jenny Garrett to attract more Black coaches. Jenny is a well-known coach, speaker, author and activist on the issue of bringing more diversity to the coaching community. Jenny says that our conversation helped spur her into setting up the Diverse Executive Coach Directory, which is an excellent initiative as it showcases the many Black and minority ethnic coaches out there that may have been overlooked in the past.

Since then, we have proactively diversified our coach team both in terms of gender and ethnicity. Our Rocket Girl coach Mary Doyle (Mary flies light aircraft in her spare time, hence the soubriquet), has enriched my thinking about how we go about fixing the system and ensure we are not 'fixing the women'. As Mary says, '[F]ixing the women is like the medical model of disability which focuses on impairment and being cured, whereas the social model recognises that society, including negative attitudes, creates the barriers, and it needs to change to embrace difference.'

A good example is adjusting our language and describing Mary as 'a wheelchair user' rather than 'confined to a wheelchair'. The fact she's learned to fly is a testament to how Mary doesn't confine herself to anything. She likes to 'rock her difference', and as she put it, she 'might not be everyone's cup of tea but she could be someone's double vodka!'

I feel that I have learned so much by embracing difference and our coach team is much the stronger for it. But having a more diverse team is just one step of the journey, because it is one thing to invite people to a party but it's quite another for them to feel they can join in the dancing. You will have noticed the slight change to this now well-known quote. It was originally 'it's quite another to invite them to dance'. I've changed it to reflect that including people is about making people feel like they belong and to do that you need to engender the psychological safety that makes them want to join in, without necessarily having to be invited.

In conclusion

I have covered how inclusive leadership is more than a set of skills, and instead it's a set of principles that underlie behaviour. As such, it's important to embark on a journey inwards with the coachee to discuss what they hold dear. I have outlined a three-circle model to help frame this journey showing how the self, our relationships with others and different systems form a dynamic interaction through which we walk in partnership with our coachee. As we walk with them, we encourage them to loosen any tightly held assumptions and see that by embracing ambiguity they are welcoming in more possibilities. And finally, I have applied a systemic lens and seen how the same challenges at play in the wider system are reflected in the coaching profession and in my own company.

You will have noticed that I haven't touched on gender much at all in this penultimate chapter. I've shifted my focus to leaders and their accountability for being inclusive. And being inclusive takes in a much broader sweep of diversity and recognises that leaders will require multiple perspectives to face the complex challenges ahead. They must embrace different ethnicities and races and take in the perspective of the significant proportion of people who are denied easy access to work, whether it's because they use a wheelchair or are neurodivergent. It's no longer acceptable or sensible for business to focus exclusively on the views of white males. In my final chapter, I will return to the theme of why there are so few women leaders and consider what is it about the current system of work that might be at the root of the exodus of women from the leadership track.

Some good coaching questions

Self

1 What drives you?
2 What inspires you?
3 What makes you happy?
4 What do you enjoy doing?
5 What gets you down?
6 How do you get yourself out of a low?
7 What thinking patterns do you default to?
8 What habits have you acquired?
9 What threatens you?
10 What triggers you?
11 What have you always been good at?
12 What are you working on getting better at?
13 What area of expertise do you offer, what do you know a lot about? What do you want to learn?

Others

1 What are you known for?
2 What differentiates you?
3 How do you communicate with others?
4 What characterises your interactions, with your inner circle, with those less close to you?
5 How are you perceived in conflict situations?
6 How do you influence?
7 Are you more prone to a push style of influence or a pull style?
8 How does your influence differ with those dependent upon where they sit in relation to the hierarchy?
9 How do you use your power?

10 How does your self-view correspond to others' views of you? Who do you gravitate towards? Who do you overlook?

11 Who do you avoid?

System

1 How are the challenges of the world impacting your role?
2 What do you believe in?
3 What do you value?
4 What's your purpose?
5 How aware are you of the systems in which you're operating?
6 Are you part of the in-group or the out-group?
7 Which stakeholders are taking precedence and which are being overlooked?
8 What changes do you want to see happen in the world? How does your job enable you to contribute to change on a broader scale?

10 The real culprit

Every day I'm simply trying to get to the end of the day and when I get to Friday it's such a relief. Saturdays I'm spending all day in bed, scrolling on my phone. It's got to the point that when I'm asked what I think I no longer know what I think.

These are not the words of a teenager. They came from a 45-year-old male CEO who has been working punishing hours for the last five years and has just landed his dream job. The only problem is now that he's got it, he hasn't got the energy or enthusiasm to do it, let alone enjoy it. He's realised that until now he was driven by getting to the next level, but now that he's got to the top his sense of purpose has disappeared. He's suffering from burnout, which is the other pandemic we're all coping with today.

When I think about how we can resolve the problem of why so few women, all roads lead back to how we tackle the culture of overwork that is prevalent today. I had always thought that flexible working was the silver bullet. If people, i.e. women, i.e. mothers, had more autonomy over how and when they worked, then they would be able to balance their lives and stay on the career track. I'm aware that not all women are mothers and so the problem goes deeper than simply their availability, but I did think that more flexibility could make significant inroads into resolving the problem. However, the experience of lockdown may have exacerbated the problem for women. It has shown in technicolour the reality for many that our jobs are dominating too much of our lives and often, in the swirl of trying to get it all to work, women are defaulting to carrying the load at home. And when that becomes too much it's often women who elect to step back from paid work. Perhaps we need to tackle the problem from a different angle. We need to look at what causes the 'swirl of trying to make it all work' in the first place.

History of the 'work ethic'

It's interesting to examine the roots of this culture of overwork that seems so prevalent today. It's not a new phenomenon. The expression a 'good work ethic' can be traced back to the Reformation in the 1600s when Protestantism emerged to challenge the predominant religion of Catholicism. The principal tenet that Protestants challenged was the supremacy of the church as the only channel to God. Instead, Protestants believed that individuals could have their own relationship with God, which detracted from the supremacy of the church as an all-powerful organ of divine power.

This is the genesis of the individualism that eventually morphed into being the political bedrock of Western democratic thinking. At its core is the idea that every individual has free will and the ability to make of their lives what they will. This provoked a focus on hard work as the means to bettering oneself. Hence the expression a 'Protestant work ethic'. Fast forward a few centuries and this individualistic approach, where people are encouraged to feel they can do anything if they set their mind to it, was at the core of the American Dream, which spawned a great consumer boom.

Despite the prescience shown by F. Scott Fitzgerald in *The Great Gatsby* in 1925, four years before the Wall Street Crash, when he highlighted the inequality wrought by Western capitalism, that cocktail of consumerism and individualism still prevails today. As I write, the Olympics are on and every English-speaking gold medallist when interviewed about their success trots out the mantra that 'you can achieve your dreams as long as you work hard at it'. Malcolm Gladwell's best-selling book *Outliers* (2009) highlights that most successful people have got to where they are based on the number of hours they've spent learning their craft. Ten thousand hours is the requisite practice period for becoming an expert. This is effectively laying down a challenge for us all to work hard and we will succeed.

Individualism questioned

The problem is it doesn't acknowledge that we don't have the same opportunity to put in the hours or the same access to what's needed to succeed. It doesn't acknowledge the influence of the system. It doesn't acknowledge that there are in-groups and out-groups where people feel marginalised by the system. This is important because those that believe in this individualistic model are more prone to a 'fix the women' solution than a 'fix the system' approach. I take you back to the law firm managing partner who asked, 'What system?' or my QC dinner companion who didn't believe there was any bias in the judiciary. What's worrying is that the belief that if you work hard you will succeed seems ever more pronounced today. And it's not just the beneficiaries of the system that buy into it. Too many of the people I coach resort to working even harder to try to resolve problems that are intrinsically systemic. Unfortunately, the outcome of this is all too often burnout, like what has happened to my aforementioned CEO.

Hard work intensified

I believe that since the post-war boom a couple of trends have coalesced to intensify the focus on hard work as the 'be-all and end-all'. The gradual breakdown of organised religion in the Western world has left a gap in terms of the community it fosters and the provision of a higher purpose. Social media has replaced physical communities with online communities, with consumerism as the driving force. As churches have lost some of their social relevance, consumerism driven by big corporates has stepped in to take their place.

It's as if we now worship at the altar of extreme work, forgoing our personal time in our efforts to be seen to be successful. And the nature of that success has changed too. It's not just about having a good job. The concept of a job which allowed you to work to live has changed. It transmuted into having a career, which is about living to work, and now it has morphed into having a calling. And that calling requires extreme dedication and total focus.

The gig economy – some misgivings

I was recently interviewed on a men's radio station to talk about burnout. I was paired with a young man who held very different views from me. He seemed to me to be boasting about how he survives on four hours sleep a night and positively relishes an extreme work ethos. He was completely dismissive about my concerns about burnout. It was like being transported back to the 1980s Gordon Gekko days of Wall Street where the main protagonist uttered the immortal line, 'Lunch is for wimps'.

Of course, he may have just been taking a provocative stance for the sake of radio, but it was perhaps also significant that he was a freelancer, in other words part of the snappily titled 'gig economy'. Unlike Gordon Gekko, he didn't have the back up of a big corporate to assure his livelihood. There's no doubt that the gig economy fuels insecurity, driving people to even forgo sleep to focus on work. Perhaps my fellow guest on the radio show was simply putting a positive spin on what was, in reality, a necessity?

That said, I do feel that young people are influenced by social media, which seems to fetishise hard work. But it's not just any work or any job, it's the dream job which is 'meaningful' and allows you to 'self-actualise'. To be frank, I think there's undue pressure in your twenties to find the 'dream job', particularly so early in your career when you need to meander a bit to figure things out. And if their day jobs don't provide the opportunity to self-actualise, young people are exhorted to develop a 'side hustle' in addition to their day jobs, making them even busier. This quest for meaning encourages them to convert their side hustle into a start-up in which they can create their own culture, one that isn't hampered by the perceived boomer anachronisms of careers and presenteeism. And yes, it's true that at 34 that's precisely what I did, but nonetheless, I agree with Derek Thompson who, when writing for The Atlantic, made the excellent point that:

> 'There is something slyly dystopian about an economic system that has convinced the most indebted generation in American history to put purpose over paycheck. Indeed, if you were designing a Black Mirror labor force that encouraged overwork without higher wages, what might you do?'

He goes on to suggest that you would exaggerate the importance of purpose and play down the importance of money. It's a fairly cynical view but I think there's something in it. Whilst I do sympathise with young people who are turning their backs on monolithic organisations that are resistant to change, I fear for them too. (Thompson, 2019)

The trouble with this re-framing of what work means is that it requires people to be devoted not just committed, rather like a religion in fact. And to be devoted you have to give all your time, which is fine when you're in your twenties and fired up by the 'living the dream' vision of success, but it's less appealing when you have a mortgage, bills to pay and a family to take care of.

So how will 'big corporate' fare?

This presents corporations with two problems. They are losing some of the cream of the grad population, who are being attracted to the start-up world and to big tech which bears the hallmarks of the gig economy with their cool workspaces and professed unlimited leave policies. The people that remain, often locked in by the regular paycheck, have care-giving responsibilities which they find hard to juggle with the 'always-on' culture of large international companies and their 'follow the sun' attitude to time zones.

The zeal for the '24/7 employee' leads to situations such as a recruitment consultant being briefed to find someone for a role and specifically instructed not to put forward any 'breeders'! (OK, this was five years ago, I can't imagine that happening now.) But it is still manifest in websites such as 'Pregnant Then Screwed', where women divulge their stories of being made redundant or having their jobs given away while on maternity leave. Clearly, it's very hard to compete with people who can devote their entire lives to their job and that extends beyond women to anyone with a personal life. It's not helped by macho tweets like this from Elon Musk, the Tesla and SpaceX CEO: '... *nobody ever changed the world on 40 hours a week*' (Musk, 2018).

Recent prominent figures in financial services have also been extolling the virtues of the 72-hour week, with one American banker describing how graduates should expect to work 12-hour days and six days a week to really master their jobs (Erdoes, 2021). There's also the case of the graduate analysts of another US investment bank who wrote anonymously to their CEO asking for a reduction in their punishingly long hours only to be met with an offer of more money (Hewitson, 2021).

Work is not home

It seems that an 'ideal worker' is someone who is available at all times with no personal responsibilities to get in the way. Women may be the ones that overtly struggle with this mantra when it comes to having a family, but it's men, and women without children, who have to keep up the pretence that they're available at all hours despite them sharing a desire to have a rich personal life. In the recent past, companies, mainly tech companies, have gone as far as to provide sleep pods, concierge services and free meals all in a bid to encourage workers to think of work as their home and their colleagues as their work families. And yet this ethos of life/work integration is somewhat disingenuous because it's conditional upon sustained high performance and, more importantly, total availability. If you fall short, there's no security because a job for life is not part of this new psychological contract.

The working from home revolution spawned by the pandemic has certainly hastened the death knell of presenteeism by proving that work does get done remotely. However, although presenteeism may have abated, the long-hours culture appears to still be endemic with workers having simply swallowed up the commuting time which repeated lockdowns afforded with more online meetings. So, what will it take to have companies curb the punishingly long hours that help suppress the number of women prepared to go all in to make it into leadership?

The growing awareness of the link between overwork and mental health

Despite my previously stated misgivings about young people's resistance in the face of the lure of the system, I do have some hope that the generation coming into the workplace has a far greater understanding of and respect for the importance of mental wellbeing. In the light of an ever-growing prevalence of poor mental health, with more people than ever before reporting signs of anxiety, depression and burnout, young people are beginning to challenge this all work and no play approach. Corporate leaders are befuddled by younger people's self-imposed 'rules' around how much time they're prepared to commit to the day job. The young investment bank analyst revolt is evidence of that. There's also evidence that they are taking steps towards engaging in the self-compassion that I spoke about in the last chapter, which will help them prioritise mental health over long hours.

Headspace

The adoption of the app Headspace by over 200 million people worldwide is testimony to a new interest in mindfulness and the importance of mental health. Andy Puddicombe, a former monk and meditation expert, has brought his mission to improve the health and happiness of the world to the mainstream. Many of the same companies that are promoting long-hours cultures are simultaneously providing free access to Headspace. One might question the intentions behind this. If they truly believe in better mental health, surely they would do better to change the long-hours culture? Are Headspace and similar benefits being provided as a prop to ensure they continue being able to handle the pressure?

Research that highlights that performance dips after repeated weeks of working longer than 52 hours is beginning to gain traction (Merle, 2021).

What we now know about the deleterious effects of sleeplessness on judgement should worry companies who are trading on the judgement skills of their workforce. Consultants, lawyers and all those in the professional classes need to pay heed to this. We humans are simply more prone to errors when we don't get enough rest and we have a greater tendency to get lost in the weeds.

If this isn't enough to grab the attention of those companies still extolling a culture of extreme work, what might do the trick are recent studies in the USA that have shown a marked interest in employees' expectations of companies' responsibility for mental health. A 2020 study of 1,000 American workers showed that 80 per cent said they 'would consider quitting their current position for a job that focused more on employees' mental health' (Westfall, 2020). A similar picture showed up in a 2021 UK study of employees with only 16 per cent of people in the study feeling very well supported by their employer when it comes to their mental health and yet 81 per cent of study participants registered that they want employers to support mental wellbeing (Davies, 2021). Interestingly, this rose even further to nearly all (99 per cent) young men between 16 and 24 years old wanting their employers to support mental wellbeing. In the same study, 40 per cent said they'd change jobs if their employer did not support their mental wellbeing.

There needs to be a focus on output over input

As companies fight over an ever-discerning talent pool, they will have to do more than offer subscriptions to Headspace to attract the best workers. They will have to get better at 'equating work with output rather than input'. While this expression has been circulating for some years, I don't think it's been successfully translated into action by many of the companies in which I coach. It's these companies in which women have been first to eschew cultures that appear to favour those who are seemingly available 24/7. Having children strikes me as a pivotal point in the realisation that all is not well, but it requires women on both sides of this juncture to come together to provide their support to push for the changes that are necessary, to push for a new 'bridge' which would benefit everyone. And of course, it requires men to also be engaged in pushing for this shared vision of a better future.

So, what can coaches do?

Most of us are working in cultures that are transitioning towards a fairer, more inclusive business model and the individuals within these companies are all themselves at different points in this journey. I coach some leaders who are keen to make such a transition and want help in understanding how they can become more output focused now that they feel more inclined to trust that the work will get done even if they're not in the same room. I coach global leaders who have been managing remotely for years and so they are more practised, and their focus is on how to maintain engagement over distance. And I coach some that are casualties themselves of extreme work and are desperate for help to re-focus.

In every coaching assignment, I meet the individual where they are at. I enquire what's brought them to coaching and often they express concern about the long-hours culture that they are working in and the rising levels of stress. In this respect, I find common ground with most leaders. They too feel that they are victims of the long-hours culture as much as their employees

Take my leader at the start of this chapter. It's as if he's got into the groove of long hours following a period of intense activity, but hasn't managed to find the off button now that things have quietened down. He is continuing to do the long hours even though he knows it's having a detrimental effect on his personal relationships and is beginning to take its toll on his mental health.

Although there are certainly macro trends, as I've outlined earlier, which have got us to where we are now, there are also many psychological factors that can hold someone hostage to a culture they themselves might find unsupportable. In the case of my stressed leader, it's a complex cocktail of ego, insecurity, trust issues, habit and now apathy triggered by exhaustion that prevents him drawing the boundaries necessary for good mental health and a good life. As I have shown in the previous chapter, the coaching need is to start with the self and examine how he can practise more self-compassion. It's about helping him to sort through multiple, often competing, demands, and take a systemic approach to analyse inter-dependencies and help simplify his priorities. In doing this I'm looking to empower people to take control and ownership over their way of working while empathising with their feelings of being overwhelmed brought on by the culture of extreme work.

I see the coach role is to support leaders by:

- Building their confidence to map out their own priorities in the face of often conflicting pressures and role model how to manage boundaries in order to signal it's OK for staff to do likewise
- Helping them to think systemically and consider competing demands with a more objective lens, bringing to light some of the emotional triggers which might be provoking anxiety-led overwork
- Encouraging them to build a culture that does not see long hours and constant availability as a proxy for commitment, but instead focuses on output over input
- Inspiring men to partake in caregiving as there's evidence that it's good for them (Palkovitz, 2014), it's good for their kids (Burgess and Davies, 2017) and it's good for society overall because it makes men happier and it maximises women's potential in the workforce (Burgess, n.d.).

In this way, coaching can make a significant impact by helping to cultivate a world of work that is conducive to those who wish to have both a rich personal life and a career, which is surely a world we all want.

Time for a reset

But perhaps it's time for an even greater reset. It's certainly our role as coaches to help people cope, but are we merely helping to re-arrange the deck chairs on the Titanic? As the bigger issues of global warming and rising inequality, which our current system is causing, continue to spiral, I wonder if we as coaches have a role in asking more demanding questions of the leaders we coach?

Let me return to Hettie Einzig (2017), whom I quote in Chapter 6: '[W]hether leader or coach it behooves us to choose our values and our position towards the world, our work and our purpose' (p. 49). My guiding purpose and remit is focusing on having more women in leadership, but I can see this is simply one measure of success in a far more ambitious vision of a fairer world. As coaches, the greater challenge is surely in helping leaders to realise the value in being more inclusive in order that we can achieve that fairer world. And that would mean more radical change than ceding some power to women. It would mean re-thinking our economic model, which seems to me to favour the few on the back of the hard labour of the rest, and advocate for a more equitable and sustainable model.

Companies are already struggling to reconcile competing and sometimes contradictory objectives. How do we make profit to make shareholders happy but also not take short cuts that might drive profit but put too much pressure on our staff or harm the environment? In this scramble to keep all the plates spinning, there's ever more pressure on staff to go the extra mile but over time that has a cumulative effect on mental wellbeing. The pandemic, along with the onslaught of major climactic catastrophes we see in the news on a daily basis, may have led people to reassess what's important.

My feeling is that an emphasis on family values and a back-to-basics, possibly less materialistic philosophy will emerge among those professional classes that are working these punishing hours. The shift to virtual working has meant that employees are less emotionally tethered to companies now that they no longer offer the same opportunities for human engagement. This focus on 'what really counts', and by that I mean what is emotionally nourishing, will have more people questioning the long-hours/high-rewards psychological contract and employers will inevitably lean into what their people need.

As coaches I see our role as helping our clients to get in touch with their own humanity, which inevitably means engaging with the broader themes affecting all lives today. Since corporates appear to be taking over the mantle of power from sovereign states or governments, I can see how we, as coaches to corporate leaders, are at the nexus of that power and uniquely placed to have a positive impact.

In this way, we can help our clients through our coaching to be agents of the change that helps to usher in cultures that are more conducive to people's lives in general, which will ultimately result in more women leaders.

Bibliography

Chapter 1

Alliance for Board Diversity (2021) *Missing Pieces Report: The Board Diversity Census of Women and Minorities on Fortune 500 Boards, 6th edition*. Deloitte. Available at: www2.deloitte.com/content/dam/Deloitte/us/Documents/center-for-board-effectiveness/missing-pieces-fortune-500-board-diversity-study-sixth-edition.pdf (accessed 6 August 2021).

Anon. (2011) Ethnicity facts and figures. GOV.UK. Available at: www.ethnicity-facts-figures.service.gov.uk/ (accessed 29 November 2021).

Anon. (2020) New Parker Review report reveals 'slow progress' on ethnic diversity of FTSE boards. EY UK. Available at: www.ey.com/en_uk/news/2020/02/new-parker-review-report-reveals-slow-progress-on-ethnic-diversity-of-ftse-boards (accessed 29 November 2021).

Catalyst (2021) Homepage. Catalyst. Available at: www.catalyst.org/ (accessed 30 November 2021).

Davies, E.M. (2011) *Women on Boards*. GOV.UK. Available at: https://assets.publishing.service.gov.uk/government/uploads/system/uploads/attachment_data/file/31480/11-745-women-on-boards.pdf (accessed 20 September 2021).

Ditzler, J. (1993) *The Executive Coach* (Television Series).

Dixon-Fyle, S. et al. (2020). Diversity wins: How inclusion matters. McKinsey. Available at: www.mckinsey.com/featured-insights/diversity-and-inclusion/diversity-wins-how-inclusion-matters (accessed 10 November 2021).

ECC (n.d.) Homepage. Available at: www.executive-coaching.co.uk/ (accessed 12 May 2022).

Fine, C. (2010) *Delusions of Gender: The Real Science Behind Sex Difference*. London: Icon Books Ltd.

HR Dive (2018) The HR profession's big diversity question: Where are the men? Available at: www.hrdive.com/news/the-hr-professions-big-diversity-question-where-are-the-men/542611/ (accessed 14 November 2021).

Jablonska, J. (2021) Seven charts that show COVID-19's impact on women's employment. McKinsey & Company. Available at: www.mckinsey.com/featured-insights/diversity-and-inclusion/seven-charts-that-show-covid-19s-impact-on-womens-employment (accessed 29 November 2021).

Marcus, J. (2017) Why men are the new minority in college. *The Atlantic*, August. Available at: www.theatlantic.com/education/archive/2017/08/why-men-are-the-new-college-minority/536103/ (accessed 29 November 2021).

Partridge, J. (2021) Number of FTSE 100 female directors rises by 50% in five years. *The Guardian*, 23 February. Available at: www.theguardian.com/business/2021/feb/23/number-of-ftse-100-women-directors-rises-by-50-in-five-years (accessed 29 August 2021).

Peterson, J.B. (2019) *12 Rules for Life: An Antidote for Chaos*. London: Penguin.

Rogers, J. (2012) *Coaching Skills: A Handbook*. Maidenhead: McGraw-Hill/Open University Press.

Vinnicombe, S. et al. (2021) *The Female FSTE Board Report*. EY. Available at: www.cranfield.ac.uk/som/research-centres/gender-leadership-and-inclusion-centre/female-ftse-board-report (accessed 2 November 2021).

Chapter 2

Anon. (2011) Project Implicit. Available at: https://implicit.harvard.edu/implicit/selectatest.html (accessed 23 November 2021).

Baron-Cohen, S. (2012) *Essential Difference: Men, Women and the Extreme Male Brain.* London: Penguin.

BBC Stories (2017) *Girl Toys vs Boy Toys: The Experiment – BBC Stories.* YouTube. Available at: www.youtube.com/watch?v=nWu44AqF0iI.

Bittman, M., et al. (2003) When does gender trump money? Bargaining and time in household work. *American Journal of Sociology,* 109(1): 186–214.

ECC (2020) *The Working Parents Change4Good Quiz.* Executive Coaching Consultancy. Available at: https://executive-coaching.co.uk/ecc-articles/change4good/?utm_source=Newsletter&utm_medium=referral&utm_campaign=Change4GoodQuizHB (accessed 10 February 2022).

ECC (2021) *Parents-To-Be: Quiz.* Executive Coaching Consultancy. Available at: https://executive-coaching.co.uk/work-family-you/thinking-ahead/parents-to-be-quiz/ (accessed 23 November 2021).

Einzig, H. (2017) *The Future of Coaching: Vision, Leadership and Responsibility in a Transforming World.* Abingdon, Oxon: Routledge.

Financial Times (2021) Investing in the menopause can offer many rewards. *Financial Times,* 19 August. Available at: www.ft.com/content/e5929095-75d1-4bf8-a434-52165ced1a95 (accessed 10 February 2022).

Fine, C. (2010) *Delusions of Gender: The Real Science Behind Sex Difference.* London: Icon Books Ltd.

Fine, C. (2017) *Testosterone Rex: Unmaking the Myths of Sex of Our Gendered Minds.* London: Icon Books Ltd.

Gallacher, G. and Petriglieri, J. (2021) *Shifting the Needle Podcast, Episode 4: Dual-career Couples.* Available at: www.executive-coaching.co.uk/videos-podcasts/shifting-the-needle-episode-4/ (accessed 9 May 2022).

Hanish L.D. and Fabes R.A. (2014) Peer socialization of gender in young boys and girls, in Tremblay, R.E., Boivin, M. and Peters, R.DeV. (eds) *Encyclopedia on Early Childhood Development.* Available at: www.child-encyclopedia.com/gender-early-socialization/according-experts/peer-socialization-gender-young-boys-and-girls (accessed 14 February 2022).

Mainiero, L.A. and Sullivan, S.E., (2006) *The Opt-out Revolt: Why People are Leaving Companies to Create Kaleidoscope Careers.* Mountain View, CA: Davies-Black.

Mainiero, L.A. and Gibson, D.E. (2017) The Kaleidoscope career model revisited. *Journal of Career Development,* 45(4): 361–77. Available at: https://journals.sagepub.com/doi/abs/10.1177/0894845317698223.

Petriglieri, J. (2019) *Couples That Work: How to Thrive in Love and at Work.* London: Penguin Life.

Petriglieri, J. (2020) *How Working Couples can Best Support Each Other.* Ted.com. Available at: www.ted.com/talks/jennifer_petriglieri_how_working_couples_can_best_support_each_other?language=enon (accessed 14 February 2022).

Prime, J.L., Carter, N.M. and Welbourne, T.M. (2009) Women 'take care,' men 'take charge': Managers' stereotypic perceptions of women and men leaders. *The Psychologist-Manager Journal,* 12(1): 25–49. Available at: http://cbafiles.unl.edu/public/cbainternal/facStaffUploads/women%20take%20care.2009.published.pdf (accessed 9 September 2019).

Samman, E. et al. (2016) Women's work: mothers, children and the global childcare crisis. ODI. Available at: https://odi.org/en/publications/womens-work-mothers-children-and-the-global-childcare-crisis/ (accessed 23 November 2021).

Tannen, D. (2013) *You Just Don't Understand: Women and Men in Conversation.* London: Virago.

Webber, A. (2021) Paternity leave hit 10-year low during pandemic. *Personnel Today*, 23 August. Available at: www.personneltoday.com/hr/paternity-leave-at-10-year-low/ (accessed 10 February 2022).

Chapter 3

Anderson, C. (2020) Why do women make such good leaders during COVID-19? *Forbes*, 19 April. Available at: www.forbes.com/sites/camianderson1/2020/04/19/why-do-women-make-such-good-leaders-during-covid-19/?sh=69c187a042fc (accessed 10 February 2022).

Catalyst (2007) *The Double-Bind Dilemma for Women in Leadership: Damned if You Do, Doomed if You Don't (Report).* Available at: www.catalyst.org/research/the-double-bind-dilemma-for-women-in-leadership-damned-if-you-do-doomed-if-you-dont/ (accessed 17 June 2021).

ECC (2015) *Women and the City – How Employers Can Attract and Retain Female Talent for the Future.* Executive Coaching Consultancy. Available at: https://executive-coaching.co.uk/ecc-articles/women-and-the-city/ (accessed 11 February 2022).

Harney, D. (2021) Optimising persuasive impact: Pull and Push – but Pull first! GPB. Available at: www.gpb.eu/2021/09/optimising-persuasive-impact-pull-and-push-but-pull-first.html (accessed 10 February 2022).

Sandberg, S. (2014) *Lean in: Women, Work, and the Will to Lead.* London: Allen.

Sasson, D. (2021) *Are There Gender Differences in Goal Setting?* The Faculty of Industrial Engineering & Management. Available at: https://web.iem.technion.ac.il/site/are-there-gender-differences-in-goal-setting/ (accessed 14 February 2022).

Schein, V.E. (1973) The relationship between sex role stereotypes and requisite management characteristics. *Journal of Applied Psychology*, 57(2): 95–100.

Syed, M. (2021) *Rebel Ideas: The Power of Diverse Thinking.* London: John Murray.

Whitmore, J. (1992) *Coaching for Performance: A Practical Guide to Growing Your Own Skills.* London: Nicholas Brealey.

Williams, J.E. and Best, D.L. (1990) *Measuring Sex Stereotypes: A Multination Study* (Rev. ed.). London: Sage.

Zenger, J. and Folkman, J. (2021) Research: Women are better leaders during a crisis. Zenger Folkman, 7 January. Available at: https://zengerfolkman.com/articles/research-women-are-better-leaders-during-a-crisis/ (accessed 9 May 2022).

Chapter 4

Blackett, K. and Mills, E. (2020) *Purpose & Allyship – Podcast.* Available at: www.linkedin.com/video/live/urn:li:ugcPost:6800396690777092096/ (accessed 15 September 2021).

Brewer, M. B. and Gardner, W. (1996) Who is this 'we'? Levels of collective identity and self representations. *Journal of Personality and Social Psychology*, 71(1): 83–93. doi:10.1037/0022-3514.71.1.83

Byers, D. (2021) Nursery costs soar above £7,000 a year during Covid pandemic. *The Times*. Available at: www.thetimes.co.uk/article/nursery-costs-soar-above-7-000-a-year-during-covid-pandemic-8ngl57qv5 (accessed 14 February 2022).

Carey, C. (2021) Returning to Work after Childbirth: An Exploration of Mothers' Experiences in the United Kingdom. Masters Dissertation. University of Salford, Salford.

Ditzler, J. (1993) *The Executive Coach* (Television Series).

Eagly, A. H. (2005) Achieving relational authenticity in leadership: Does gender matter? *The Leadership Quarterly*, 16: 459–74. doi:10.1016/j.leaqua.2005.03.007

ECC (2015) *Women and the City – How Employers Can Attract and Retain Females*. Executive Coaching Consultancy. Available at: https://executive-coaching.co.uk/ecc-articles/women-and-the-city/ (accessed 16 August 2021).

García, H. and Miralles, F. (2017) *Ikigai: The Japanese Secret to a Long and Happy Life*. London: Hutchinson.

Ibarra, H. (2004) *Working Identity: Unconventional Strategies for Reinventing Your Career*. Boston, MA: Harvard Business School Press.

Kimmel, M.S. and Aronson, A. (2008) *The Gendered Society Reader*. New York: Oxford University Press.

Kliff, S. (2015) 1 in 4 American moms return to work within 2 weeks of giving birth – Here's what it's like. *Vox*. Available at: www.vox.com/2015/8/21/9188343/maternity-leave-united-states (accessed 11 November 2021).

Noon, H. and van Nieuwerburgh, C. (2020) Looking forward to going back? The experience of career decision-making for first-time mothers and the implications for coaches. *International Journal of Evidence Based Coaching and Mentoring*, 18(1): 88–102.

Oppenheim, M. (2019) Children raised by single mothers are achieving less because of lower income, study finds. *The Independent*, 20 November. Available at: www.independent.co.uk/news/uk/home-news/children-single-mothers-acheive-less-grades-jobs-low-income-a9210576.html (accessed 3 November 2021).

Pascale, R., Sternin, J. and Sternin, M. (2010) *The Power of Positive Deviance*. Boston, MA: Harvard Business Press.

Petriglieri, J. (2020) *How Working Couples can Best Support Each Other*. Ted.com. Available at: www.ted.com/talks/jennifer_petriglieri_how_working_couples_can_best_support_each_other?language=enon (accessed 14 February 2022).

Sealy, R.H.V. and Singh, V. (2010) The importance of role models and demographic context for senior women's work identity development. *International Journal of Management Reviews*, 12: 284–99. doi:10.1111/j.1468-2370.2009.00262.x

Schein, V.E. (1973) The relationship between sex role stereotypes and requisite management characteristics. *Journal of Applied Psychology*, 57(2): 95–100.

Skinner, S. (2014) Understanding the importance of gender and leader identity formation in executive coaching for senior women. *Coaching: An International Journal of Theory, Research and Practice*, 7(2): 102–14.

Chapter 5

Clance, P.R. and Imes, S.A. (1978) The imposter phenomenon in high achieving women: Dynamics and therapeutic intervention. *Psychotherapy: Theory, Research & Practice*, 15(3): 241–7. Available at: https://psycnet.apa.org/record/1979-26502-001 (accessed 3 November 2021).

Exley, C. and Kessler, J. (2019) The gender gap in self-promotion. NBER. Available at: www.nber.org/papers/w26345 (accessed 29 May 2021).

Guillén, L. (2017) For women, self-confidence not enough for workplace success. *Forbes India*, 9 July. Available at: www.forbesindia.com/article/esmt/for-women-selfconfidence-not-enough-for-workplace-success/47457/1 (accessed 24 March 2021).

Kay, K. and Shipman, C. (2014) *The Confidence Code: The Science and Art of Self-assurance – What women should know*. New York, NY: Harper Collins.

Lakoff, R. (1973) Language and Woman's Place. *Language in Society, 2*(1): 45–80. Available at: www.jstor.org/stable/4166707

Mahoney, N. (2019) Modesty does not become her. Eureka Street. Available at: www.eurekastreet.com.au/article/modesty-does-not-become-her# (accessed 11 March 2022).

Mainiero, L.A. and Sullivan, S.E. (2006) *The Opt-out Revolt: Why People are Leaving Companies to Create Kaleidoscope Careers*. Mountain View, CA: Davies-Black.

Sandberg, S. (2014) *Lean in: Women, Work, and the Will to Lead*. London: Allen.

Tannen, D. (2013) *You Just Don't Understand: Women and Men in Conversation*. London: Virago.

Thomson, S. (2018) A lack of confidence isn't what's holding back working women. *The Atlantic*. Available at: www.theatlantic.com/family/archive/2018/09/women-workplace-confidence-gap/570772/ (accessed 29 November 2021).

Valenti, J. (2014) Women don't need 'choreplay'. They need men to do some chores. *The Guardian*, 23 April. Available at: www.theguardian.com/commentisfree/2014/apr/23/female-confidence-gap-katty-kay-claire-shipman (accessed 19 February 2021).

Zenger, J. and Folkman, J. (2019) Research: Women score higher than men in most leadership skills. *Harvard Business Review*, June. Available at: https://hbr.org/2019/06/research-women-score-higher-than-men-in-most-leadership-skills (accessed 18 June 2021).

Chapter 6

Brown, B. (2010) *The Power of Vulnerability*. Ted.com. Available at: www.ted.com/talks/brene_brown_the_power_of_vulnerability?language=en (accessed 4 September 2020).

Changingminds.org (n.d.) *Rogers' Five Feedback Types*. Available at: http://changingminds.org/techniques/conversation/reflecting/rogers_feedback.htm (accessed 4 November 2021)

Einzig, H. (2017) *The Future of Coaching: Vision, Leadership and Responsibility in a Transforming World*. Abingdon, Oxon: Routledge.

Kline, N. (2002) *Time to Think: Listening to Ignite the Human Mind*. London: Cassell Illustrated.

Marien, B. (2018) *The Importance of Psychological Wellbeing*. Available at: www.positivegroup.org/loop/articles/the-importance-of-psychological-wellbeing-an-interview-with-dr-brian-marien (accessed 17 February 2021).

Shabi, A. and Stevens, L. Available at: www.linkedin.com/posts/leadership-coach_climatechange-friendship-coaching-activity-6870764476057034752-S1Eo/ (accessed 3 May 2021).

Yalom, Irvin D. (n.d.). *Books*. Available at: www.yalom.com/books (accessed 10 February 2022).

Chapter 7

Anon. (n.d.) Patriarchy. *The Oxford Pocket Dictionary of Current English*. Available at: www.encyclopedia.com (accessed 12 July 2020).

Bohnet, I. (2018) *What Works: Gender Equality by Design*. Cambridge, MA: The Belknap Press of Harvard University Press.

Britannica (2018) Homeostasis. *Encyclopædia Britannica*. Available at: www.britannica.com/science/homeostasis (accessed 4 November 2021).

Clark, K.B. and Clark, M.P. (1950) Emotional factors in racial identification and preference in Negro children. *The Journal of Negro Education*, 19(3): 341–50. Available at: https://doi.org/10.2307/2966491 (accessed 4 February 2021).

ECC (n.d.) *Women in the Workplace – Six Stages of a Woman's Career*. Executive Coaching Consultancy. Available at: https://executive-coaching.co.uk/women-in-the-workplace/ (accessed 15 February 2022).

Erikson, E.H. (1993) *Childhood and Society*. New York: W.W. Norton & Company. Available at: www.sas.upenn.edu/~cavitch/pdf-library/Erikson_EightStages.pdf (accessed 13 May 2021).

MacBride, E. (2021) Women need sponsors, not mentors. *Forbes*, 8 November. Available at: www.forbes.com/sites/elizabethmacbride/2021/11/08/women-need-sponsors-not-mentors/?sh=545192b8339e (accessed 10 February 2022).

Mainiero, L.A. and Sullivan, S.E. (2006) *The Opt-out Revolt: Why People are Leaving Companies to Create Kaleidoscope Careers*. Mountain View, CA: Davies-Black.

Maitland, A. and Steele, R. (2020) *INdivisible: Radically Rethinking Inclusion for Sustainable Business Results*. Canada: Young & Joseph Press.

Nielsen, T.C. and Kepinski, L. (2020) *Inclusion Nudges Guidebook: 100 Practical Techniques: Designs based on behavioural insights: How you can de-bias and change your organisations and society to be inclusive as the default and the norm*. North Charleston, SC: CreateSpace.

Sandberg, S. (2014) *Lean in: Women, Work, and the Will to Lead*. London: Allen.

Wallace, D.F. (2005) This is water. Commencement speech at Kenyon College. Available at: https://fs.blog/david-foster-wallace-this-is-water/

Chapter 8

Bond, E. (2018) Benevolence bias – are you being cruel by being kind? LinkedIn. Available at: www.linkedin.com/pulse/benevolence-bias-you-being-cruel-kind-elanor-bond (accessed 26 January 2021).

Cotter, K. (2016) *Attitudes of Coachees, Line-Managers and HR Leaders Toward Maternity Coaching*. Available at: https://optimisecoaching.co.uk/onewebmedia/Attitude of coachees.pdf (accessed 29 March 2021).

ECC (2021) *Surrogacy*. Executive Coaching Consultancy. Available at: https://executive-coaching.co.uk/work-family-you/thinking-ahead/surrogacy/ (accessed 10 February 2022).

Fairygodboss (2019) Engaging male allies. Jobs, Company Reviews, Career Advice and Community. Available at: https://fairygodboss.com/presentation/male-allies-research (accessed 26 September 2020).

Kimmel, M. (2015) *Why Gender Equality is Good for Everyone – Men Included.* Ted.com. Available at: www.ted.com/talks/michael_kimmel_why_gender_equality_is_good_for_everyone_men_included?language=en (accessed 10 November 2021).

Prime, J. and Moss-Racusin, C.A. (2009) The Goldman Sachs Group, Inc. Available at: www.catalyst.org/research/engaging-men-in-gender-initiatives-what-change-agents-need-to-know/ (accessed 17 July 2020).

Sutherland, R. (2018) Tackling the root causes of suicide. NHS Choices. Available at: www.england.nhs.uk/blog/tackling-the-root-causes-of-suicide/ (accessed 26 June 2021).

Tabor, D., Stockley. L. (2018) Personal well-being in the UK: October 2016 to September 2017. Personal well-being in the UK. Available at: www.ons.gov.uk/peoplepopulationandcommunity/wellbeing/bulletins/measuringnationalwellbeing/october2016toseptember2017 (accessed 26 October 2020).

Chapter 9

Anon. (2017) Inclusive leadership. The Ocean Partnership. Available at: www.theoceanpartnership.com/blog/inclusive-leadership (accessed 26 November 2021).

Bortini, P. et al. (2016) *The Inclusive Leadership Handbook: Theoretical Framework.* Available at: https://inclusiveleadership.eu/the-inclusive-leadership-handbook-theoretical-framework/ (accessed 9 May 2021).

Brooks, A.C. (2022) How to want less. *The Atlantic*, March. Available at: www.theatlantic.com/magazine/archive/2022/03/why-we-are-never-satisfied-happiness/621304/ (accessed 14 February 2022).

Brown, B. (2018) *Dare to Lead: Brave Work, Tough Conversations, Whole Hearts.* New York: Random House.

ECC Insights (2021) Empathy – The missing link to inclusion. Executive Coaching Consultancy. Available at: https://executive-coaching.co.uk/ecc-articles/empathy-the-missing-link-to-inclusion/ (accessed 8 July 2021).

Edmondson, A. (2014) *Building a Psychologically Safe Workplace.* YouTube. Available at: www.youtube.com/watch?v=LhoLuui9gX8&ab_channel=TEDxTalks (accessed 26 November 2021).

Gilbert, P. (2020) Compassion: From its evolution to a psychotherapy. *Frontiers in Psychology,* 11(586161). https://doi.org/10.3389/fpsyg.2020.586161

Jenny Garrett Global (n.d.) Home page. Available at: www.jennygarrett.global/ (accessed 10 January 2021).

Neff, K. (2011) *Self Compassion: Stop Beating Yourself Up and Leave Insecurity Behind.* London: Yellow Kite.

Oxford Dictionary (2022) Philosophy. *Oxford Advanced Learner's Dictionary.* Available at: www.oxfordlearnersdictionaries.com/definition/english/philosophy

Chapter 10

Burgess, A. (n.d.) *Evidence and Insights to Inform the Development of Policy and Practice: The Costs and Benefits of Active Fatherhood. Sponsored by: A paper prepared by Fathers Direct to inform the DfES/HM Treasury Joint Policy Review on*

Children and Young People. Available at: www.fatherhoodinstitute.org/uploads/publications/247.pdf (accessed 14 February 2022).

Burgess, A. and Davies, J. (2017) *Cash or Carry?* Available at: www.fatherhoodinstitute.org/wp-content/uploads/2017/12/Cash-and-carry-Full-Report-PDF.pdf (accessed 14 February 2022).

Davies, R. (2021) UK workers feel pressure to hide mental health concerns, survey finds. *The Guardian,* 4 August. Available at: www.theguardian.com/business/2021/aug/04/uk-workers-feel-pressure-to-hide-mental-health-concerns-survey-finds (accessed 26 October 2021).

Einzig, H. (2017) *The Future of Coaching: Vision, Leadership and Responsibility in a Transforming World.* Abingdon, Oxon: Routledge.

Erdoes, M. (2021) Junior bankers need to work 12 hour days to master their jobs. *Bloomberg,* 20 July. Available at: www.bloomberg.com/news/videos/2021-07-20/new-bankers-need-to-work-72-hours-a-week-j-p-morgan-s-erdoes-says-video (accessed 26 July 2021).

Gladwell, M. (2009) *Outliers: The Story of Success.* London: Penguin.

Hewitson, J. (2021) When money isn't enough to justify 90 hours a week. *The Times,* 8 Augsut. Available at: www.thetimes.co.uk/article/when-money-isnt-enough-to-justify-90-hours-a-week-qnnxxfh28 (accessed 26 October 2021).

Merle, A. (2021) This is how many hours you should really be working. Work Life by Atlassian. Available at: www.atlassian.com/blog/productivity/this-is-how-many-hours-you-should-really-be-working (accessed 26 November 2021).

Musk, E. (2018) Twitter, 26 November. Available at: https://twitter.com/elonmusk/status/1067173497909141504?lang=en (accessed 26 November 2021).

Palkovitz, R. (2014) *Involved Fathering and Men's Adult Development.* Hove: Psychology Press.

Thompson, D. (2019) Workism is making Americans miserable. *The Atlantic,* February. Available at: www.theatlantic.com/ideas/archive/2019/02/religion-workism-making-americans-miserable/583441/ (accessed 26 November 2021).

Westfall, C. (2020) Mental health and remote work: survey reveals 80% of workers would quit their jobs for this. *Forbes,* 8 October. Available at: www.forbes.com/sites/chriswestfall/2020/10/08/mental-health-leadership-survey-reveals-80-of-remote-workers-would-quit-their-jobs-for-this/?sh=3fc766413a0f (accessed 6 November 2021).

Index

Page numbers in *italics* are figures.

www.ingramcontent.com/pod-product-compliance
Lightning Source LLC
Chambersburg PA
CBHW061257220326
41599CB00028B/5684